Ukraine: A Historical Atlas

Publication of this volume was made possible through the

generosity of Peter Jacyk who, in cooperation with the

Chair of Ukrainian Studies at the University of Toronto,

wishes to commemorate the beginning of the second millennium

of Christianity in Ukraine-Rus' with this cartographic survey of

three millennia of Ukrainian history.

UKRAINE : A Historical Atlas

PAUL ROBERT MAGOCSI

Geoffrey J. Matthews, cartographer

UNIVERSITY OF TORONTO PRESS

Toronto Buffalo London

© University of Toronto Press 1985
Toronto Buffalo London
Printed in Canada
ISBN 0-8020-3428-4 (cloth)
ISBN 0-8020-3429-2 (paper)

Canadian Cataloguing in Publication Data

Magocsi, Paul R.
   Ukraine, a brief historical atlas
   (University of Toronto Ukrainian studies; no. 1)
   Includes index.
   ISBN 0-8020-3428-4 (bound).—ISBN 0-8020-3429-2 (pbk.)
   1. Ukraine – Historical geography – Maps.
   2. Ukraine – History. I. Matthews, Geoffrey J., 1932–
   II. Title. III. Series.

   G2151. S1M34 1985   911′.4771   C85-099602-3

MAY '86

CONTENTS

Preface

1 Geography of the Ukrainian lands
2 Ethnolinguistic setting of the Ukrainian lands
3 Greek colonies and the steppe hinterland
4 Eastern Europe, 250–800
5 East Slavic and adjacent tribes in the ninth century
6 Trade routes in medieval Europe
7 Kievan Rus' in the eleventh century
8 Southern Rus' circa 1250
9 Ukrainian lands circa 1400
10 Ukrainian lands after 1569
11 Zaporozhia
12 Ecclesiastical divisions in the sixteenth and
     seventeenth centuries
13 The Cossack state after 1649
14 Ukrainian lands after 1667
15 Ukrainian lands circa 1750
16 The Russian Empire in Europe
17 The Dnieper Ukraine, 1850
18 Minority populations in nineteenth-century Ukraine
19 The Austro-Hungarian Empire
20 Western Ukraine, 1772–1914
21 Ukrainian lands, 1914–1919
22 Ukrainian lands during the interwar years
23 Ukrainian lands during World War II
24 Ukrainian Soviet Socialist Republic since World War II
25 Index map and gazetteer

Sources

PREFACE

During the past two decades, a marked increase in Ukrainian studies has occurred in North America. Several universities now offer courses in Ukrainian history, language, and literature, and a few like Alberta, Harvard, and Toronto have endowed chairs or research institutes in Ukrainian subjects. At the secondary level, especially in Canada's western provinces, Ukrainian language and culture courses are offered as part of the provincial educational curriculum. Alongside this growing interest in Ukrainian matters has arisen the need for adequate textbooks and other pedagogical materials designed for English-speaking students.

This atlas is one response to the practical demand for university-level and advanced secondary pedagogical materials related to Ukrainian subjects. It is, therefore, modest in scope and does not pretend to fulfill the need for a comprehensive atlas of Ukrainian history, which has yet to be published either within or beyond the Ukrainian homeland. Maps 3 through 24 in this atlas follow basically chronological developments in Ukraine from earliest times to the present. By Ukraine or Ukrainian lands is meant both the present-day Ukrainian Soviet Socialist Republic and Ukrainian ethnolinguistic territory, that is, contiguous lands within and beyond the Ukrainian SSR where Ukrainians live.

Like most other countries, Ukraine has experienced varying periods of political discontinuity. This means that, like Belgium, Poland, Italy, or Germany, for instance, Ukraine might not have existed in its present form or even as a concept during long periods in the past. Yet, the histories of those countries from earliest times according to their present-day boundaries—and Ukraine is no exception—are legitimate subjects of study.

The name Ukraine was only one of many used in the past to designate all or part of present-day Ukrainian lands. The other commonly used designations were Rus' and Little Russia. In the medieval period, the name Rus' (the Rus' Land / *Rus'ka Zemlia* / Ruthenia) was most widely

used, although after the sixteenth century that term was preserved for the most part in western Ukrainian lands (Galician Rus' / Red Rus', or in ecclesiastical circles, Little Rus' / *Mikrá Rosía* / *Mala Rus'*), surviving by the mid-twentieth century only in the farthest western Ukrainian region (Transcarpathian or Subcarpathian Rus'). In the late sixteenth century, the term Ukraine was used for the first time to delineate a specific territory: the eastern Ukrainian lands under Polish rule. This concept of Ukraine was maintained during the seventeenth century by the Cossack state and was used as well by western observers, such as the French geographer Guillaume de Beauplan. The seventeenth century also witnessed a revival of the old ecclesiastical concept, Little Rus', although this time in the form Little Russia (*Malorossia*), in order to designate those Ukrainian Cossack lands that were joined to Muscovy as well as other Ukrainian lands subsequently incorporated into the Russian Empire. By the twentieth century, especially following the struggle for independent statehood after World War I, the name Ukraine was used again to designate all Ukrainian lands.

In order to provide a continuous perspective with the present, the boundaries of the Ukrainian SSR are indicated on each map as well as, when necessary, the political boundaries and Ukrainian ethnolinguistic boundaries appropriate to the particular period. Also, for comparative purposes, an effort has been made to maintain consistency throughout the atlas with regard to the use of color, cartographic symbology (international, provincial, ethnographic, historic boundaries), and place-names (countries, provinces, regions). Each of the maps is accompanied by a brief commentary describing the events that occurred during the time frame depicted. The emphasis in this atlas is on political and administrative boundary changes, although some geographic, cultural, and military developments are indicated as well.

Place-names are generally rendered according to the language of the country in which they are now located. Therefore, Ukrainian forms are used for places within the Ukrainian SSR. On the other hand, the Polish form appears for Przemyśl (Ukrainian: Peremyshl'), because even though that city is within Ukrainian ethnolinguistic territory, it is located within the present-day political boundaries of Poland. A few commonly accepted English names (Kiev, Odessa, Cracow, Podolia, Zaporozhia, etc.) are retained in those more well-known forms. Finally, historic names, such as those for Greek and Roman cities during the pre-Slavic era, or older names for still existing places (Stanyslaviv, Katerynoslav, Stalino) are retained for the periods during which they were used.

The gazetteer that accompanies Map 25 provides names of towns, cities, regions, and other place-names that appear within most of the Ukrainian ethnolinguistic territory covered on the other 24 maps. The grid numbers help to locate the given item, which then can be found on one or more of the maps throughout the book.

I am very grateful to Geoffrey Matthews, chief cartographer of the University of Toronto's Department of Geography, for his design and to cartographers Chris Grounds, Hedy Later, Jane Davie, and Ada Cheung for their skill and patience in producing the maps. The maps are based on data provided by the author and taken from a wide variety of sources, most especially those studies listed at the back of the book. Much appreciation is extended to Bohdan Budurowycz (University of Toronto), Lubomyr Luciuk (University of Toronto), and Jaroslaw Pelenski (University of Iowa), who reviewed the material during the pre-publication process and made valuable suggestions for revisions. Responsibility for the final result, however, rests with me alone.

PRM
Toronto, March 1985

Ukraine: A Historical Atlas

MAP 1

Geography of the Ukrainian lands

There are two types of Ukrainian territory: political and ethnographic or ethnolinguistic. Political territory refers to lands within the present-day boundaries of the Ukrainian SSR (232,200 square miles / 601,000 square kilometers), which makes it larger than any European country except Russia and approximately the size of Manitoba in Canada or Arizona and New Mexico combined in the United States. Ukrainian ethnolinguistic territory refers to all contiguous lands within and just beyond the Ukrainian SSR that are inhabited by Ukrainians (288,800 square miles / 747,500 square kilometers), which cover an area approximately the size of Alberta and New Brunswick in Canada or Texas in the United States.

The geographic setting for both Ukrainian political and ethnolinguistic territory is not complex and may be divided into five topographic zones. These zones run more or less in parallel belts extending from west to east: (1) the belt of mountains including the Carpathians in the west and the Crimeans in the south; (2) the belt of coastal lowlands on the Black Sea Lands from the mouths of the Danube to the northern shore of the Sea of Azov and including the northern Crimea and the lowland north of the Kuban River; (3) the central plateau and upland belt including much of Volhynia, eastern Galicia, and Podolia, which is connected by the ridges of Zaporozhia to uplands farther east in the Donbas; (4) the belt of northern lowlands, from the marshes of Polissia through northern Volhynia, and including lands east of the Dnieper River to the northeastern boundary of the Ukrainian SSR; (5) the East European upland north of the Ukrainian SSR / Russian SFSR boundary as far east as the Don River.

Most of these topographic zones consist of plains and plateaus that do not exceed 500 meters in altitude. Higher elevations are found only in the extreme west and south, but these account for no more than 5 per cent of the total Ukrainian land surface. The highest peaks are Hoverla (2,061 meters) in the Carpathians and Roman Kosh (1,543 meters) in the Crimean Mountains.

Ukrainian territories have a well-knit network of major rivers with tributaries belonging to two watersheds. Most rivers are part of the Pontic watershed and flow in a southeasterly or southwesterly direction into the Black Sea or Sea of Azov. From west to east, these include the Dniester, Boh, Dnieper (with its major tributaries, the Pripet and Desna), and the Donets', a tributary of the Don

that empties into the Sea of Azov. The major rivers in the far northwestern Ukraine, the San and Buh, belong to the Baltic watershed and flow in a northwesterly direction into the Vistula, which eventually empties into the Baltic Sea.

The Baltic and Pontic watersheds are rather closely interlinked in the western Ukraine, so that historically they have become part of an important communication network that has made possible trade from the Baltic Sea through Poland via the Vistula and Dniester rivers down to the Black Sea (see Map 8). The Pontic watershed has also made communication possible with the north, that is, via the upper reaches of the Dnieper which come close to major Belorussian and Russian rivers and cities, thus facilitating direct communication from the Baltic Sea and Gulf of Finland to the Black Sea (see Map 6: Trade routes in medieval Europe). It is along or near these rivers that the oldest and newer major Ukrainian cities have been established. In the west, Przemyśl (Peremyshl') on the San and L'viv are close to tributaries of the Buh and Dniester, which therefore provide access to both the Baltic and Black seas. In central and eastern Ukraine, the most important centers have been Chernihiv on the Desna, a tributary of the Dnieper; Kiev, Cherkasy, and the newer Dnipropetrovs'k and Zaporozhia along the Dnieper; and Kharkiv near the Donets'. To the south, Mykolaïv is at the mouth of the Boh and the major Black Sea port of Odessa is near the mouth of the Dniester.

Minsk

BELORUSSIAN
S.S.R.

Western Dvina

Buh

PODLACHIA

Warsaw

POLAND

Brest

Pinsk

Pripet

POL'ISSIA

Tambov

EAST EUROPEAN UPLAND

Dnipro

Desna

Voronezh

Kursk

Chernihiv

Chełm

Vistula

VOLHYNIA

San

U. S. S. R.

RUSSIAN

Zhytomyr

Kiev

NORTHERN LOWLANDS

SLOBODA UKRAINE

S. F. S. R.

GALICIA

Przemyśl

L'viv

UKRAINIAN

Bila Tserkva

S. S. R.

Kharkiv

Poltava

Don

CZECHOSLOVAKIA

CARPATHIAN

Uzhhorod TRANSCARPATHIA

CENTRAL

Cherkasy

Donets

Chernivtsi

Dniester

PODOLIA

Dnipropetrovs'k

DONBAS

HUNGARY

+ Hoverla

BUKOVINA

MOUNTAINS

MOLDAVIAN S.S.R.

PLATEAU

Tysa

Prut

BESSARABIA

Buh

Kryvyi Rih

Zaporozhia

ZAPOROZHIA

Donets'k

Rostov

COASTAL

BLACK SEA LANDS

Mykolaiv

LOWLANDS

KALMYK A.S.S.R.

—··— International boundaries, 1985

——— Soviet Socialist Republic boundaries

- - - Autonomous Soviet Socialist
Republic boundaries

Odessa

SEA OF
AZOV

KUBAN

Kuban

Elevation

	3000 m
	2000
	1000
	500
	200
	Sea level

ROMANIA

DOBRUDJA

CRIMEA

REGION

Krasnodar

Bucharest

Scale 1: 6 300 000

0   50   100   150 Miles

0   50   100   150 Kilometers

Sevastopil'

CRIMEAN MTS.

Roman Kosh

Yalta

Danube

BLACK SEA

CAUCASUS MTS.

KABARDINO-
BALKAR
A.S.S.R.

GEORGIAN S.S.R.

MAP 2

Ethnolinguistic setting of the Ukrainian lands

Although the Ukrainian SSR is at present divided into 25 oblasts (see Map 24), it is the historic regions which have been of greatest importance in the past. The names of these areas are also frequently used to describe the regional identity of the Ukrainian inhabitants and, in some cases, they are also used to classify ethnographic and linguistic groups (for example, Galicians or Galician Ukrainians, Bukovinians).

Among the most important historic regions are Volhynia, Galicia, Transcarpathia, Podolia, the Sloboda Ukraine, Zaporozhia, the Donbas, the Black Sea Lands, and the Crimea. Other regions which are wholly or partly inhabited by Ukrainians and which are wholly or partly within neighboring states are: the Lemkian Region, the San Region, the Chełm (Kholm) Region, and Podlachia in the west; Polissia in the northwest; Bukovina, Bessarabia, and the Danubian delta in the southwest; and the Don Valley and Kuban Region in the east. There are two other somewhat less specific entities which have frequently appeared in historical writing: the Left Bank Ukraine, or simply the Left Bank, and the Right Bank Ukraine, or simply the Right Bank. The Left Bank is the region east of the Dnieper River, as far as the Sloboda Ukraine in the east and Zaporozhia in the south. The Right Bank is the region west of the Dnieper and includes most of Volhynia and Podolia.

With regard to population, in 1979 the Ukrainian SSR had 49,609,000 inhabitants. Of these, 36,490,000 (73.6 per cent) were Ukrainian. There were also an estimated 6,747,000 more Ukrainians living in contiguous ethnolinguistic territory just outside the borders of the Ukrainian SSR: in the Belorussian SSR within the marshland of the Pripet River valley; in Poland along its eastern border in the Podlachia, Chełm, San, and Lemkian regions; in Czechoslovakia in the Prešov region of northeastern Slovakia; in Romania in the Maramarosh and northern Moldavian regions and Danubian delta; in the Moldavian SSR throughout the Bessarabian Plain; and in the Russian SFSR along the Don and Kuban River Valleys and in the region east of the Sea of Azov (see also Map 24).

TABLE I
Ukrainians outside the Ukrainian SSR
(on contiguous ethnolinguistic territory)

Belorussian SSR	191,000
Poland	150,000
Czechoslovakia	100,000
Romania	100,000
Moldavian SSR	506,000
Russian SFSR	5,700,000
Total	6,747,000

As for the 13,119,000 inhabitants (26.4 per cent) belonging to ethnic or national minorities within the Ukrainian SSR, the vast majority are Russians (21.1 per cent), who live in compact areas in the Donbas and in industrial centers along the lower Dnieper as well as in very high proportions in the Crimea. The other minorities include Jews and Belorussians, mostly in urban industrial areas; Moldavians in southern Podolia and southern Bessarabia; Poles spread throughout Volhynia and eastern Galicia; Bulgarians in southern Bessarabia and along the northern shore of the Sea of Azov; Hungarians in southern Transcarpathia; Greeks just north and west of Zhdanov on the Sea of Azov; and Tatars in the Crimea. (See Map 18 for minority population distribution in the nineteenth century.)

TABLE II
Ethnic Composition of the Ukrainian SSR, 1979

Group	Number	Percentage
Ukrainians	36,490,000	73.6
Russians	10,472,000	21.1
Jews	634,000	1.3
Belorussians	406,000	0.8
Moldavians	294,000	0.6
Poles	258,000	0.5
Bulgarians	238,000	0.5
Hungarians	164,400	0.3
Greeks	104,100	0.2
Tatars	90,500	0.2

The language spoken by Ukrainians can be divided into three major dialect groups: northern, eastern, and western. The eastern group covers the largest geographic area and has the least internal dialectal differentiation. The western dialect group contains the largest number of dialectal sub-groups, with great differentiation especially in its westernmost regions both within and beyond the boundaries of the Ukrainian SSR, including the San, Lemkian, Boikian, Transcarpathian, Hutsul, Pokuttian, and Bukovinian dialects.

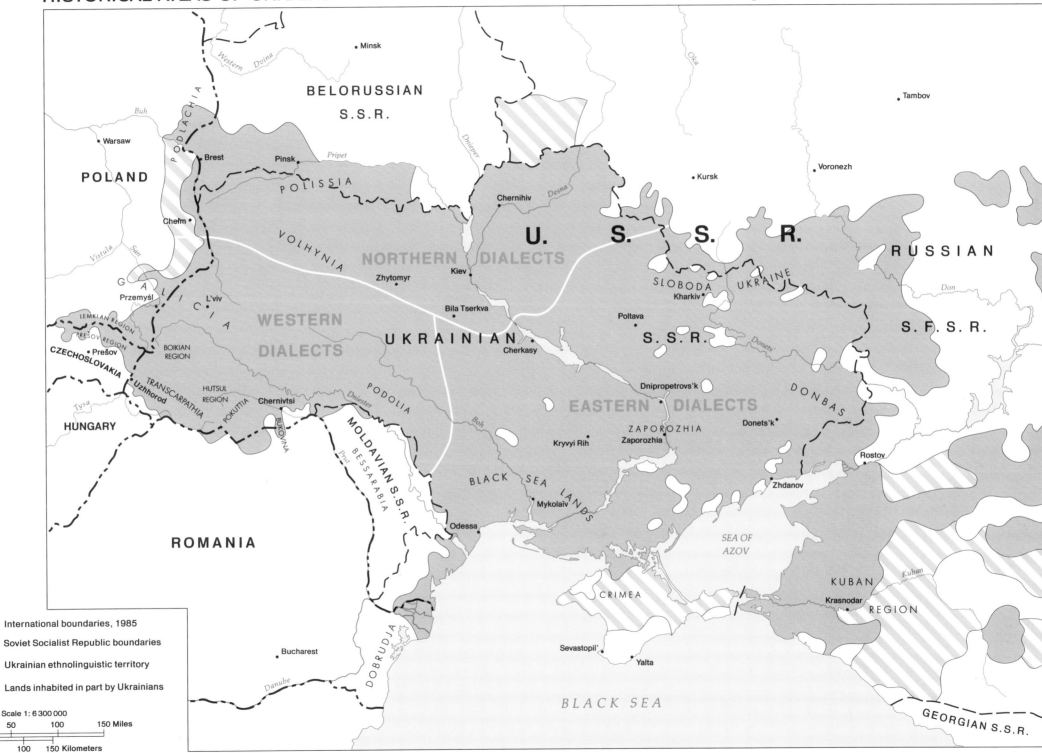

POLAND

BELORUSSIAN S.S.R.

- Minsk
- Warsaw
- Brest
- Pinsk

Western Dvina

Buh

Pripet

P O D L A C H I A

POLISSIA

CheIm •

VOLHYNIA

G A L I C I A

Przemyśl
L'viv •

Vistula
San

WESTERN
DIALECTS

NORTHERN DIALECTS

Zhytomyr •
Kiev •

Bila Tserkva •

UKRAINIAN .

LEMKIAN REGION
PREŠOV REGION

CZECHOSLOVAKIA

• Prešov

BOIKIAN
REGION

Uzhhorod
TRANSCARPATHIA
Tysa

HUTSUL
REGION
POKUTTIA

Chernivtsi •

BUKOVINA

HUNGARY

MOLDAVIAN S.S.R.
BESSARABIA

Prut

ROMANIA

Dniester

PODOLIA

Boh

Cherkasy

EASTERN DIALECTS

Kryvyi Rih •

ZAPOROZHIA
Zaporozhia •

BLACK SEA LANDS

Mykolaïv •

Odessa •

DOBRUDJA

Danube

U. S. S. R.

• Kursk

• Voronezh

• Tambov

Oka

Dnieper

Desna

Chernihiv •

SLOBODA UKRAINE
Kharkiv •

Poltava •

S. S. R.

Dnipropetrovs'k •

Donets'k •

DONBAS

Donets'

Don

RUSSIAN

S. F. S. R.

Rostov •

Zhdanov •

SEA OF
AZOV

CRIMEA

Sevastopil' •

Yalta •

KUBAN

Krasnodar •

REGION

Kuban

BLACK SEA

GEORGIAN S.S.R.

International boundaries, 1985

Soviet Socialist Republic boundaries

Ukrainian ethnolinguistic territory

Lands inhabited in part by Ukrainians

Scale 1: 6 300 000

0   50   100   150 Miles

0   50   100   150 Kilometers

MAP 3

Greek colonies and the steppe hinterland

The appearance of the first known civilizations on Ukrainian territory dates from the first millennium BC. Much of Ukraine was inhabited by sedentary populations engaged in agriculture and livestock-raising and over whom there ruled nomadic peoples whose origins were in Central Asia. The first of these nomadic civilizations whose remains have come down to us in the form of archeological discoveries was the Cimmerian, which lasted on Ukrainian territory from about 1150 to 750 BC. The second nomadic civilization was that of the Scythians, whose sphere of influence dominated large parts of Ukrainian territory from about 750 to 250 BC. Despite their nomadic nature, the Scythians created fortified centers, such as Nemyrivs'ke, Bil's'ke, and Kamians'ke in the steppe hinterland, and Neapolis in the Crimea, where Scythian influence was still felt long after they disappeared from the steppe regions.

About the same time the Scythians appeared in the steppe hinterland, Greek colonists from the city-states of Megara and most especially Miletus established several cities along the Black Sea and Crimean coasts: Tiras, Olbia, Chersonesus, Theodosia. While these maintained a dependent or semi-dependent existence vis-à-vis the Aegean Greek mother cities, others like Panticapaeum (Bospor) and Phanagoria near the Straits of Kerch joined together to create an independent Bosporan Kingdom. This entity, which reached its first apogee between the fourth and second centuries BC, extended its influence along the eastern shore of the Sea of Azov, where it established the city of Tanais at the mouth of the Don (Tanais) River.

Both the individual Black Sea Greek colonies and the Bosporan Kingdom derived their wealth and prosperity from the symbiotic relationship that was maintained with the Scythian rulers. The Scythians extracted grain, fish, and slaves from the sedentary populace under their control and sold these to the coastal cities where they were processed and then shipped to the Greek city-states along the Aegean Sea. In turn, the Scythians purchased wine, cloth, metal objects, art works, and other luxury items from the Greeks.

The symbiotic steppe-coastal/Scythian-Greek economic relationship was disrupted after 250 BC by the arrival of Sarmatian tribes who drove out the Scythians and attacked the coastal cities.

The Scythians were forced to consolidate their rule over a smaller region, which included much of the Crimean peninsula and the lands as far north as the lower Dnieper River valley. This new political entity with its capital at Neapolis was known as Scythia Minor (*Mala Skifiia*), and it lasted from about 250 BC to AD 200. As for the larger sphere of Scythian influence in the steppe hinterland, most of this had come under the authority of the Sarmatians who, by the first century BC, had re-established the old symbiosis between the steppe and coastal cities.

Like their Scythian predecessors, the Sarmatian rulers began to ensure a steady flow of raw materials and foodstuffs to the urban centers along the coast, including those in the Bosporan Kingdom, which after 63 BC was revived under the control and protection of the Roman Empire—the Pax Romana. By the outset of the third century AD, the Bosporan Kingdom had become strong enough to defeat the Scythians and incorporate the whole Crimean peninsula under its rule. The result of these economic, political, and cultural interrelations was the evolution of a new Greek-Scythian-Sarmatian hybrid civilization under Roman hegemony that was to pervade the Bosporan Kingdom, the Crimea, and other cities along the northern shore of the Black Sea until at least about AD 250.

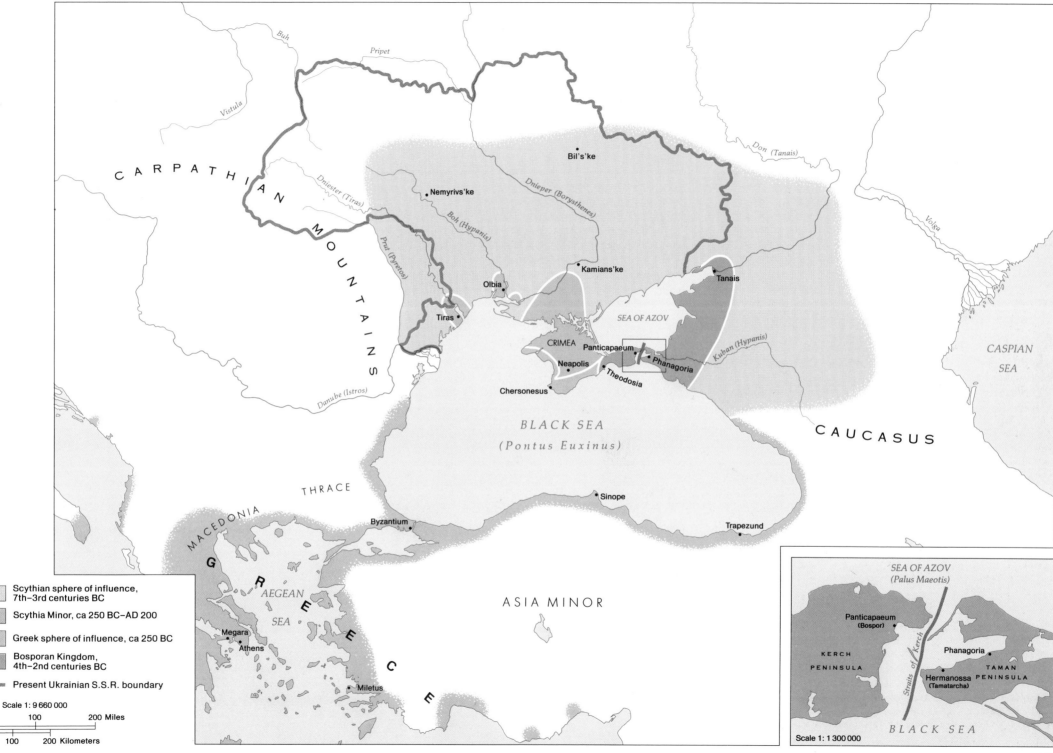

C A R P A T H I A N

M O U N T A I N S

Vistula

Buh

Pripet

Dniester (Tiras)

Prut (Pyretos)

Boh (Hypanis)

• Nemyrivs'ke

• Bil's'ke

Dnieper (Borysthenes)

Don (Tanais)

Volga

• Kamians'ke

Tanais •

Olbia •

Tiras •

Danube (Istros)

CRIMEA

Neapolis •

Panticapaeum

SEA OF AZOV

• Phanagoria

Kuban (Hypanis)

Chersonesus •

• Theodosia

CASPIAN
SEA

C A U C A S U S

BLACK SEA

(Pontus Euxinus)

• Sinope

THRACE

Byzantium •

• Trapezund

MACEDONIA

G R E E C E

AEGEAN
SEA

Megara •

Athens •

A S I A M I N O R

• Miletus

Scythian sphere of influence,
7th–3rd centuries BC

Scythia Minor, ca 250 BC–AD 200

Greek sphere of influence, ca 250 BC

Bosporan Kingdom,
4th–2nd centuries BC

Present Ukrainian S.S.R. boundary

Scale 1: 9 660 000

0   100   200 Miles

0   100   200 Kilometers

SEA OF AZOV
(Palus Maeotis)

Panticapaeum
(Bospor) •

KERCH
PENINSULA

• Phanagoria

Straits of Kerch

TAMAN PENINSULA

Hermanossa
(Tamatarcha) •

BLACK SEA

Scale 1: 1 300 000

3

MAP 4

Eastern Europe, 250–800

The seemingly invincible power of the Roman Empire and the stability it brought to the lands within its sphere of influence were seriously undermined during the third century AD. The first major disruption accompanied the arrival of the Goths from the Baltic region (between the Vistula and Nieman rivers), who descended upon Ukrainian territories about AD 150. During the third century, they attacked several Graeco-Roman coastal towns and took over the Bosporan Kingdom.

The arrival of the Goths initiated a cycle of events whose sequence was repeated several times during at least the next millennium. Nomadic warrior tribes—not however from the north, but usually from the steppes of Central Asia—were drawn by the wealth of the Roman, and later the East Roman or Byzantine, world. The invaders first entered the Kuban and Black Sea steppes, from where they exploited the local sedentary population and attacked the coastal cities. Sometimes they reached accords with the cities and re-created the steppe/coastal-city economic symbiosis that had characterized the Scythian era. Before long, however, new tribal groups would arrive from the east, often forcing the remnants of the old groups to retreat across the Roman/Byzantine *limes* (frontier) farther west into the heart of the empire or south into its fringe area, the Crimean peninsula.

The cycle of invasions and attempts to reach a modus vivendi with the Graeco-Byzantine cities was repeated several times. Following the Goths (whose Ostrogoth descendants were Christianized and survived at their center of Doros in the Crimea for several more centuries) there came from the east the Huns (ca 375), the Avars (ca 550), the Bulgars (ca 575), and the Khazars (ca 600). Of these central Asian nomadic groups, the Khazars set up the longest lasting presence centered between the lower Don, Volga, and Kuban rivers. From their capitals of Itil and later Sarkel, they created a new era of stability in the Black Sea steppe region which was to last from about the mid-seventh to mid-tenth centuries.

As for the Black Sea Greek cities, these survived as best they could against the nomadic onslaught, partially with the help of Byzantine protection, which began in earnest during the sixth century and which lasted with interruptions until the eleventh century. Also, the Bosporan Kingdom was revived under Byzantine hegemony; trade and Eastern Christian culture flourished along the coast; and generally peaceful ties were maintained with the Khazars who dominated the steppe hinterland.

Meanwhile, farther north, in an area beyond the open steppe and bounded roughly by the Carpathian Mountains to the south and encompassing the upper reaches of the Oder, Vistula, Buh (Western Buh), Dniester, Boh (Southern Buh), Pripet, and middle Dnieper rivers, a sedentary population known as Slavs survived the many onslaughts of nomadic warriors and began to expand from their original homeland. During the fifth and sixth centuries, they moved basically in three directions: farther west, farther east and northeast, and southward across the Carpathians beyond Pannonia into the mountainous areas along the Adriatic Sea and Balkan peninsula. Each branch of the Slavs was subdivided into several tribes, and several of the Eastern Slavic tribes were to establish themselves on Ukrainian territory. Some of these tribes in the western and southwestern Ukraine were even united under the name Antes and with their own rulers were able to protect themselves against invaders from both the north and east. The Antes confederation lasted from the fourth to seventh centuries.

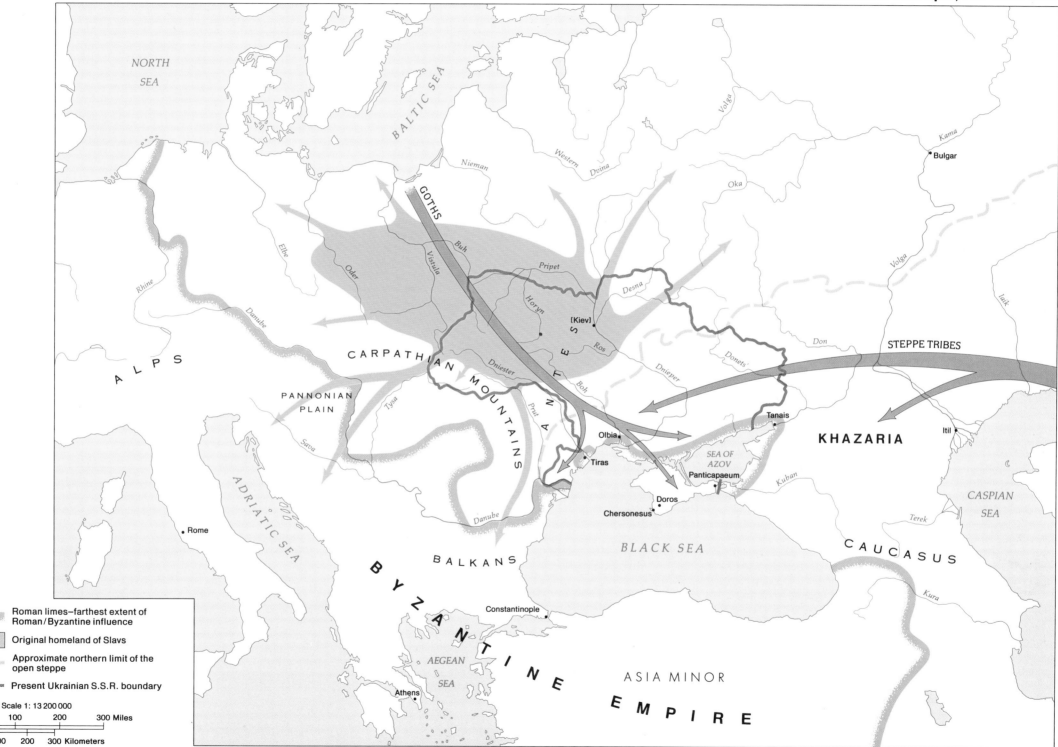

NORTH
SEA

BALTIC SEA

Nieman

Western Dvina

Volga

Oka

Kama

• Bulgar

GOTHS

Elbe

Oder

Vistula

Buh

Pripet

Desna

Volga

Rhine

Danube

Horyn

[Kiev]

Ros

STEPPE TRIBES

Iaik

CARPATHIAN MOUNTAINS

Dniester

Boh

Dnieper

Donets'

Don

A L P S

PANNONIAN
PLAIN

Tysa

A N T E S

KHAZARIA

Tanais

Sava

Prut

Olbia •

• Tiras

Itil •

ADRIATIC SEA

Danube

Doros •

Chersonesus •

SEA OF
AZOV

Panticapaeum •

Kuban

CAUCASUS

CASPIAN
SEA

Terek

• Rome

BALKANS

BLACK SEA

Kura

B Y Z A N T I N E   E M P I R E

Constantinople •

ASIA MINOR

AEGEAN
SEA

Athens •

Roman limes–farthest extent of
Roman/Byzantine influence

Original homeland of Slavs

Approximate northern limit of the
open steppe

Present Ukrainian S.S.R. boundary

Scale 1: 13 200 000

| 0 | 100 | 200 | 300 Miles |

| 0 | 100 | 200 | 300 Kilometers |

MAP 5

East Slavic and adjacent tribes in the ninth century

After the dispersal of the Slavs from their original homeland during the fifth and sixth centuries and the breakup of the Antes confederation at the outset of the seventh century, large areas of east-central and eastern Europe came to be inhabited by several tribes. The earliest documentary sources mention thirteen East Slavic tribes, seven of whom lived wholly or partially on Ukrainian territory: the Polianians, Severians, Derevlianians, Dulebians, (White) Croats, Ulichians, and Tivertsians.

The early evolution of the East Slavic tribes, especially those on Ukrainian territory, was closely linked to the development of the Khazar Empire, also known as Khazaria. The Khazars were a nomadic Turkic people from Central Asia who by the early seventh century had settled in the region between the lower Volga, Don, and Kuban rivers. Although Khazaria has subsequently become best known as the first 'state' to have converted to Judaism (its leaders had embraced that religion in the late eighth century), in the early medieval period the Khazars were most renowned for their prowess in commerce. Khazaria derived its wealth from international trade along routes that crossed its territory and which linked the Byzantine Empire (via the Black Sea), the Arab Caliphate (via the Caspian Sea), and northern Europe (via the Volga, Don, and Dnieper rivers and overland routes to the Baltic Sea)—see Map 6. In order to protect their commercial interests, the Khazars strove to maintain peace in the region and to keep out or to neutralize any new nomadic invaders from the east. They were successful in their endeavors and were able to create an era of stability in the north Pontic steppe region, known as the Pax Chazarica, which lasted from about the mid-seventh to mid-tenth centuries.

Protected by the Pax Chazarica, the East Slavic tribes north of the open steppe were able to expand farther southward and to develop further their agricultural and livestock-raising pursuits. Their traditional fortified places (known as *horody*)—originally stockades encircled by moats and ramparts—soon became small towns, where artisans produced wares (especially pottery and metal implements) and merchants conducted trade. By the ninth century, there were over one thousand *horody* on Ukrainian territory. The more important centers, which often were the home for tribal leaders or princes, were: Kiev for the Polianians, Chernihiv for the Severians, Iskorosten' for the Derevlianians, Volyn' for the Dulebians, Przemyśl for the Croats, and Peresichen' for the Ulichians.

Some of these East Slavic tribes, as well as the Viatichians and Volga Bulgars, were in a kind of economic and political vassalage to the Khazars. By the ninth century, certain East Slavic tribal leaders began to resent the Khazar overlordship and to look for ways to change their situation. One group, the Polianians, found a solution by accepting the help of Varangian military leaders and their retinues from Scandinavia, who had already been among the Slavic tribes in the north, and who, in the 860s, were invited to Kiev. This invitation to the Varangians not only resulted in the beginnings of the first long-lasting political entity among the East Slavs, it also marked the end of Khazar supremacy and the dawn of a new era in eastern European history.

NORTH
SEA

SWEDEN

Birka

Gulf of Finland

Lake Ladoga

Lake Onega

White Lake

CHUDS

VES

Staraia Ladoga

Beloozero

Lake Peipus

SLOVENIANS

MERIANS

BALTIC SEA

LETTS

Novgorod

Lake Ilmen

Lovat

Volga

DENMARK

POLOCHANIANS

Western Dvina

KRIVICHIANS

Kama

Nieman

Smolensk

BULGAR
VOLGA STATE
Bulgar
BULGARS

PRUSSIANS

Sozh

Oka

Elbe

Rhine

POLES

IATVIGIANS

Vistula

Buh

DREGOVICHIANS

Pripet

RADIMICHIANS

Desna

VIATICHIANS

Seim

Oder

Cracow

DULEBIANS

Volyn'

Styr

DEREVLIANIANS

Chernihiv

SEVERIANS

FRANKISH
EMPIRE

GREATER
MORAVIA

CROATS

Przemyśl

San

Horyn

Iskorosten'

Kiev

POLIANIANS

Ros

KHAZAR

Danube

Tysa

CARPATHIAN MOUNTAINS

Dniester

ULICHIANS

Boh

Dnieper

Don

Donets'

Sarkel
(Bila Vezha)

Volga

Prut

TIVERTSIANS

Peresichen'

EMPIRE

Itil

Sava

BULGARIAN

Danube

SEA OF
AZOV

Kuban

Tmutorokan

ADRIATIC SEA

Rome

Chersonesus

BLACK SEA

Terek

CASPIAN
SEA

EMPIRE

Preslav

CAUCASUS

BYZANTINE

Constantinople

EMPIRE

ARAB CALIPHATE

CROATS   East Slavic tribes

— · —   Approximate northern limit of the
         open steppe

══════   Present Ukrainian S.S.R. boundary

Scale 1: 13 200 000

| 0 | 100 | 200 | 300 Miles |

| 0 | 100 | 200 | 300 Kilometers |

5

MAP 6

Trade routes in medieval Europe

The establishment of Kievan Rus' in the second half of the ninth century was directly linked to international trade in eastern Europe. The Varangian Rus' traders and their accompanying military parties from Scandinavia were particularly interested in reaching the markets of the Khazar Empire along the lower Don and Volga rivers, and in receiving from there products from Central Asia (Tashkent, Bukhara, and Samarkand), the Islamic world (Baghdad), and Byzantium (Constantinople).

Setting out from Baltic ports in eastern Sweden (Sigtuna and Birka) and the island of Gotland (Visby), as early as the seventh century the Varangians reached the coastal regions of the eastern Baltic (or what became known as the Varangian) Sea and Gulf of Finland. By the ninth century they had moved farther inland and set up trading outposts like Aldeigjuborg / Staraia Ladoga, Holmgård/Novgorod, and Beloozero in the midst of Finnish and Slav tribes.

Many trading routes developed along the network of lakes and rivers of eastern Europe, all with the ultimate goal of reaching the Caspian and Black seas. In the eighth and early ninth centuries, the most important of these was the so-called Saracen route, which went up the Gulf of Finland to the southern shores of Lake Ladoga to Staraia Ladoga, and from there eastward to Lake Onega and Beloozero, eventually to reach the upper Volga. Descending the Volga, the Varangians had direct access to the strategically located capital of the Khazar Empire (Itil), connected by caravan routes to Tashkent, Bukhara, and Samarkand in Central Asia and by sea and caravan routes to Islamic Baghdad. Or, at the great bend of the Volga, the Varagians could cross over westward to the Don River and, descending it to the Sea of Azov, gain access to the Black Sea and Constantinople (or, as they called it, Miklagård), the capital and commercial emporium of the Byzantine Empire.

By the mid-ninth century, when Byzantium was becoming commercially more attractive than Khazaria, the Varangians opened up a new route, the famous route 'from the Varangians to the Greeks.' From Staraia Ladoga, it descended directly southward up the Volkhov River past Novgorod and Lake Ilmen, and continued to the upper reaches of the Lovat River. From there, the Varangian traders carried their boats southeastward (across the so-called

portage) to the upper reaches of the Dnieper River; then they sailed southward past their outpost of Smolensk and on to Kiev (which they called Könugard and which by the 860s had also come under their control). From Kiev, the Dnieper gave access to the Black Sea and across it to Constantinople. An alternative route in the north connecting the Baltic (Varangian) Sea with the Dnieper River went up the Western Dvina River past another Varangian outpost, Polotsk, and then on to the portage connecting to Smolensk.

The main object of these Varangian international trading routes through the rivers and lakes of eastern Europe was to connect the Caspian Sea (the Central Asian and Islamic worlds) and Black Sea (the Byzantine world) with the Baltic (or Varangian) Sea ports of eastern Sweden and from there to the major center of Hedeby in southern Denmark, which provided direct access to central and western Europe. Initially, the Varangians were interested in obtaining Central Asian and Islamic silver and spices in exchange for furs and slaves. After the establishment of Kievan Rus', the products of international trade were not much different from those exchanged during the Scythian/Greek coastal-city era of the millennium before Christ. Kievan Rus' basically supplied raw materials—flax, hemp, hides, slaves, honey, wax, grain, furs (from the north)—in return for luxury items like silk fabrics, naval equipment, wine, jewelry, glassware, and art items (especially icons after the introduction of Christianity) from Byzantium; or spices, precious stones, silver, silk and satin fabrics, and metal weapons from the Islamic world and Central Asia.

With the development of domestic manufactures in Kievan Rus' and the increasing menace of nomads (Pechenegs and Polovtsians) in the steppe, who hampered access to the Black and Caspian seas (see Map 7), internal trade became increasingly important beginning in the eleventh century. It was also at this time that the Crimea, the traditional source for Kiev of that all-important medieval commodity, salt, was cut off and replaced by Galicia. Thus, the overland route from Kiev westward to Halych took on increasing significance. And if Kiev's domestic market was still insufficient to meet the tastes of the upper social strata, luxury and finely manufactured products formerly from the south and east could now be received from central and western Europe via Galicia (see Map 8). Galicia's growing importance was based

on its strategic location at the crossroads of several routes that went north up the Vistula or Oder to the Baltic Sea, south over the Carpathians to Hungary, or directly west via Cracow and Prague to central Europe's foremost commercial center: Regensburg (Ratisbon).

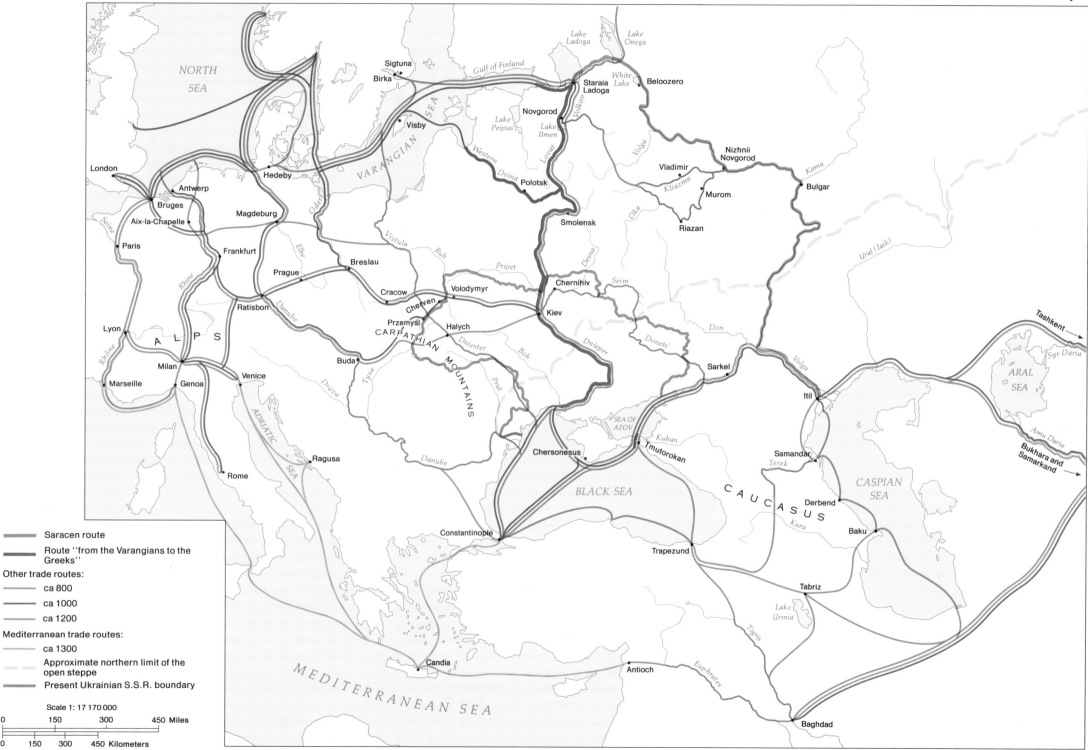

NORTH SEA

Lake Ladoga

Lake Onega

Sigtuna
Birka
Gulf of Finland
White Lake
Beloozero
Staraia Ladoga

VARANGIAN SEA

Visby

Novgorod

Lake Peipus
Lake Ilmen

Western Dvina
Lovat
Volkov
Volga

Nizhnii Novgorod

London
Hedeby
Polotsk
Vladimir
Kama
Bulgar

Antwerp
Bruges
Aix-la-Chapelle
Magdeburg
Oder
Smolensk
Oka
Murom

Seine
Paris
Frankfurt
Elbe
Breslau
Vistula
Buh
Pripet
Desna
Riazan

Rhine
Prague
Cracow
Volodymyr
Chernihiv
Seim

Ratisbon
Danube
Cherven
Przemyśl
Kiev
Don
Donets'

Lyon
Rhône
ALPS
Buda
Halych
CARPATHIAN MOUNTAINS
Dniester
Boh
Dnieper

Tashkent →

Milan
Venice
Drava
Tysa
Prut
Sarkel
Volga
ARAL SEA

Marseille
Genoa
ADRIATIC SEA
Ragusa
Danube
SEA OF AZOV
Itil

Rome

Chersonesus
Tmutorokan
Kuban
Samandar
Terek
CAUCASUS
Syr Daria

Bukhara and Samarkand →

BLACK SEA
Derbend
CASPIAN SEA
Amu Daria

Constantinople
Kura
Baku

Trapezund

Tabriz

Lake Urmia

Candia
Antioch
Tigris
Euphrates

MEDITERRANEAN SEA

Baghdad

Legend:

———— Saracen route

━━━━ Route ''from the Varangians to the Greeks''

Other trade routes:

——— ca 800

——— ca 1000

——— ca 1200

Mediterranean trade routes:

——— ca 1300

– – – Approximate northern limit of the open steppe

══════ Present Ukrainian S.S.R. boundary

Scale 1: 17 170 000

0   150   300   450 Miles

0   150   300   450 Kilometers

MAP 7

Kievan Rus' in the eleventh century

The invitation to rule extended in the 860s by certain East Slavic and other tribes from the region around Novgorod to Varangian Rus' trading and military groups led to the formation of a state structure known as Kievan Rus'. It was not long before the center of Varangian Rus' power shifted southward to Kiev. From there, Kievan Rus' came to be nominally ruled by a senior or grand prince of the Riurykovych dynasty, that is, a descendant of the semi-legendary Hroerekr (d. 879), the Varangian leader that had ruled Novgorod and was known in Rus' sources as Riuryk.

The Kievan realm consisted of several lands, or principalities, often named after a main political or administrative center which may have previously served as a center of an East Slavic tribal organization. The grand prince in Kiev generally assigned his offspring to represent him and to rule over the various principalities of Kievan Rus' that eventually stretched over a vast territory from the edge of the open steppe of Ukraine to the northern regions beyond the upper Volga River and Lakes Ladoga and Onega.

The name Rus' (itself of controversial origin) seemed to be associated both with Varangian military-trading groups and with the region around Kiev, Pereiaslav, and Chernihiv—that is, the home of the East Slavic Polianians and a branch of them known as the Ros or Rus. As the political and cultural influence of the realm expanded, so too did the concept of Rus', or the Rus' land (*Rus'kaia zemlia*), which gradually came to be identified with all the territory and inhabitants of Kievan Rus'—that is, the lands ruled by the descendants of the Riuryk dynasty and their inhabitants who, after the 980s, were officially adherents of the Christian 'Rus' faith.'

Like most medieval political entities, Kievan Rus' was not a unified state in the modern sense of the term, but rather a loosely knit group of principalities. Considering its political nature, neither the boundaries of the realm as a whole nor those of its individual principalities should be considered as definitive or fixed at any one period of time as the visual effect of historic maps would suggest. Rather, these boundaries might more appropriately be viewed as the farthest extent of a sphere or spheres of influence radiating from one or more centers of authority. Not surprisingly, these spheres of influence often overlapped, and they were continually expanding and contracting, depending on the ability of rulers at the center to enforce their authority over the inhabitants.

With regard to the Kievan realm as a whole, its influence extended farther southward before the tenth century and farther northward beginning in the twelfth century. The loss of the southern lands was related to external invasions of nomadic peoples from Central Asia, including the Pechenegs and Polovtsians in the tenth and eleventh centuries and finally the Mongols in the thirteenth century.

It was during the rule of Volodymyr the Great (reigned 980–1015) and Iaroslav the Wise (reigned 1036–1054) that Kievan Rus' experienced its greatest degree of internal cohesiveness. Thereafter, external invasions and civil wars weakened the realm, as members of the Riurykovych dynasty fought with each other for control of individual principalities and/or of Kievan Rus' as a whole. The problem of succession was never resolved, and after the death of each grand prince internecine warfare became the norm. One result was the division of the principalities into smaller units, each with its own hereditary ruling dynasty.

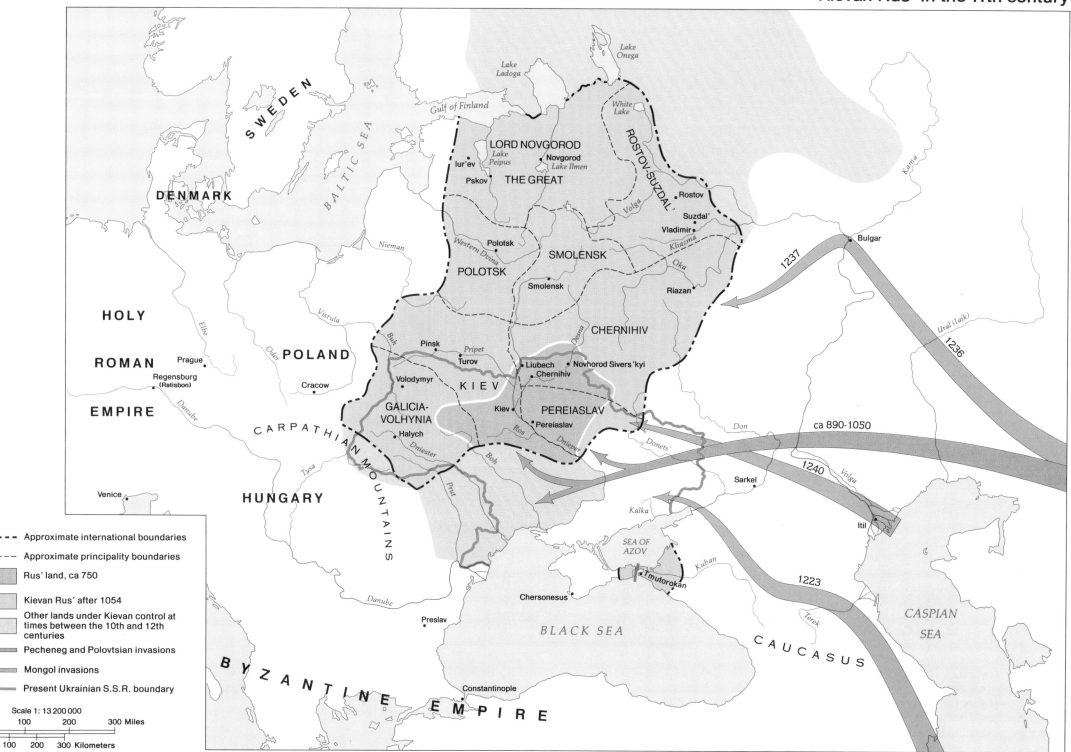

SWEDEN

DENMARK

HOLY

ROMAN

EMPIRE

Lake Ladoga

Gulf of Finland

Lake Onega

White Lake

LORD NOVGOROD

THE GREAT

Lake Peipus

Iur'ev

Pskov

Novgorod

Lake Ilmen

ROSTOV-SUZDAL

Rostov

Suzdal'

Vladimir

Volga

Kliazma

Western Dvina

Polotsk

POLOTSK

SMOLENSK

Smolensk

Oka

Riazan

Nieman

Prague

Regensburg
(Ratisbon)

Vistula

Oder

POLAND

Cracow

Buh

Pinsk

Turov

Pripet

Volodymyr

KIEV

GALICIA-
VOLHYNIA

Halych

CHERNIHIV

Desna

Liubech

Chernihiv

Novhorod Sivers'kyi

PEREIASLAV

Kiev

Pereiaslav

Ros

Dnieper

Boh

Don

Donets'

Bulgar

Ural (Iaik)

1237

1236

ca 890-1050

1240

Volga

Sarkel

Itil

Elbe

Danube

Venice

HUNGARY

CARPATHIAN MOUNTAINS

Tysa

Dniester

Prut

Danube

Preslav

Kalka

SEA OF
AZOV

Kuban

Tmutorokan

Chersonesus

BLACK SEA

1223

Terek

CAUCASUS

CASPIAN
SEA

BYZANTINE EMPIRE

Constantinople

Legend

- – ·· –   Approximate international boundaries
- - - -   Approximate principality boundaries
  Rus' land, ca 750
  Kievan Rus' after 1054
  Other lands under Kievan control at times between the 10th and 12th centuries
←   Pecheneg and Polovtsian invasions
←   Mongol invasions
  Present Ukrainian S.S.R. boundary

Scale 1: 13 200 000

0   100   200   300 Miles

0   100   200   300 Kilometers

7

MAP 8

Southern Rus' circa 1250

The process of division into distinct principalities that had begun in Kievan Rus' at the end of the eleventh century was continued, so that during the twelfth century several new entities came into existence. In the southern Rus' lands, Galicia-Volhynia split into distinct principalities; Belz was separated from Volhynia between 1170 and 1234; Turov-Pinsk was formed from northern Kiev; and Novhorod-Sivers'kyi was carved out of Chernihiv. The northern Rus' lands also changed as Murom-Riazan split off from Chernihiv, Rostov-Suzdal' became a greatly expanded entity called Vladimir-Suzdal', and Novgorod acquired control of the vast northern lands as far as the White Sea (see Map 7).

The twelfth century also witnessed the decline of Kiev as the leading political and economic focal point of the Rus' realm. By the thirteenth century, even before the Mongol invasions of 1237–1240, three new power centers had evolved: Novgorod in the far north, Vladimir-Suzdal' in the northeast, and Galicia-Volhynia in the southwest. Two of these centers, Galicia-Volhynia and Vladimir-Suzdal' (later its successor, Moscow), each claimed to be the rightful heir to the political and cultural heritage of Kievan Rus' as a whole, so that during the thirteenth and fourteenth centuries, each principality attempted to restore the albeit tenuous unity of the Kievan realm such as it had existed during the eleventh century.

The expansionist efforts of both Galicia-Volhynia and Vladimir-Suzdal' were most seriously blocked, however, by the Mongol invasions of the mid-thirteenth century (see Map 7). From their capital at Old Sarai on the lower Volga (see Map 9), the Mongols of the Golden Horde subjected all the lands of Kievan Rus' (with the exception of Polotsk and Turov-Pinsk) to their authority, and they consistently blocked any efforts at unity among the Rus' principalities.

Galicia-Volhynia had traditionally been part of a border region fought over by Rus' princes from the east and Poles from the west. The so-called Cherven cities (Brest, Chełm, Cherven, Belz) were a foremost cause of conflict since the time of their first mention in the sources (980s). It was not until the eleventh-century reign of Iaroslav the Wise that Galicia-Volhynia definitively became part of Kievan Rus'. During the twelfth century, each principality had its own branch of the Riurykovych dynasty, although

at the outset of the thirteenth century both were united under the new Romanovych dynasty established by Prince Roman (reigned 1199–1205).

Galicia-Volhynia's importance within Kievan Rus' was related to its strategic location. Straddling the headwaters of eastern Europe's two major watersheds, the region had direct access to the Baltic Sea (via the Vistula's tributaries: the Buh, Wieprz, and San rivers) and to the Black Sea (via the Dniester River). Both provinces were also crossed by major overland international trade routes which connected them to Kiev in the east; to Constantinople (via the Black Sea) in the southeast; over the Carpathian passes to Hungary in the southwest; to Poland in the west; and from there farther on to Prague and Central Europe (see also Map 6). Galicia had salt mines near its first capital, Halych, and after the steppe peoples made Crimean salt difficult to obtain, Galicia became Kiev's leading supplier of this valued medieval commodity. (Some scholars even argue that the name Galicia, in Ukrainian *Halychyna*, is derived from the Indo-European word for salt, *hal*).

Galicia-Volhynia began its real rise to power under Prince Daniel (reigned 1238–1264). He even accepted a crown from the pope (1253), so that he, as king of Rus' (*Rex Rusiae*), and his kingdom of Galicia-Volhynia (*regnum Galiciae et Lodomeriae*) became recognized as legitimate in the western European feudal order. The kingdom's growth and stability were continued under Daniel's son Lev (reigned 1264–1301), who was able to maintain good relations with the Golden Horde in the east, and from his new capital of L'viv to expand trade and commerce between east and west. Finally, in 1303, Halych was made the seat of a new Orthodox metropolitanate, which lent further cultural and religious prestige to the Galician-Volhynian state.

However, at the outset of the fourteenth century, the very apogee of Galicia-Volhynia's power and influence, the kingdom entered a period of steady decline that led to its eventual dissolution. The dying out of the Romanovych dynasty (on the male side in 1323 and female side in 1340), combined with internal dissension caused by powerful boyars and external intervention by neighboring Poland, Hungary, Lithuania, and the Mongols, weakened the kingdom beyond redemption. Finally, the years 1340 to 1387 wit-

nessed almost continuous civil war and foreign intervention, at the end of which Galicia-Volhynia ceased to exist as an independent state. In effect, the southwest Rus' lands lost their last power center. Volhynia was annexed to the Grand Duchy of Lithuania and Galicia was made part of Poland.

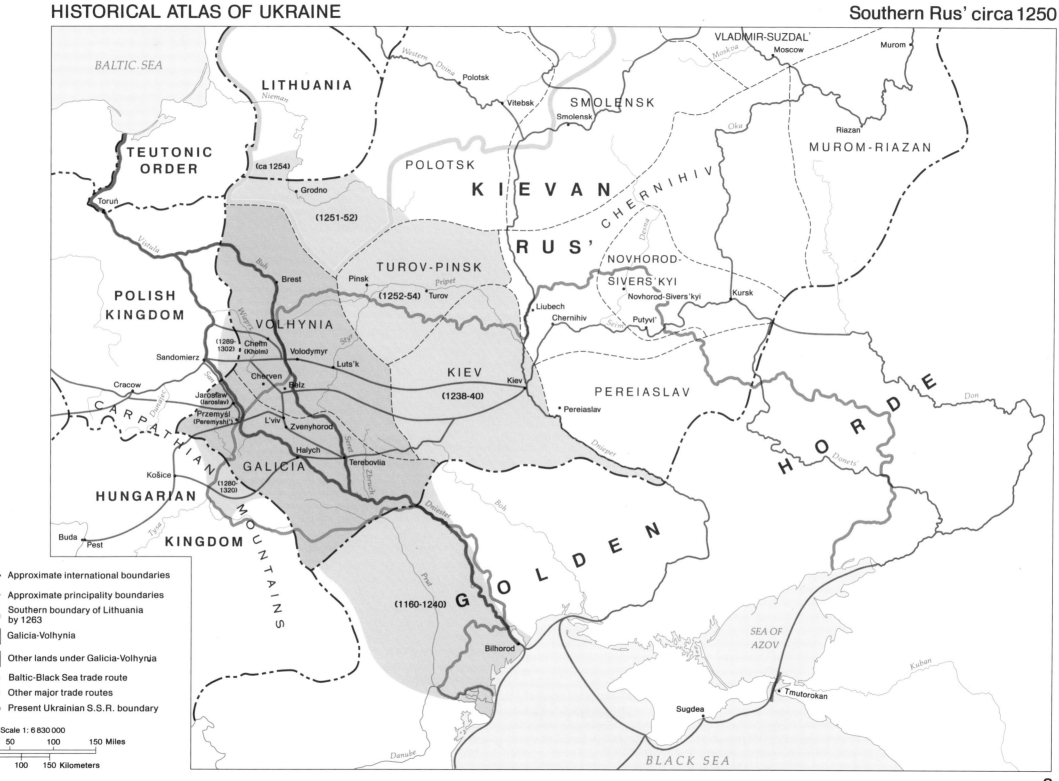

BALTIC SEA

LITHUANIA

TEUTONIC ORDER

(ca 1254)

Toruń

VLADIMIR-SUZDAL'

Moscow

Murom

Polotsk

Vitebsk

SMOLENSK

Smolensk

Grodno

POLOTSK

K I E V A N

Riazan

MUROM-RIAZAN

(1251-52)

R U S '

POLISH
KINGDOM

TUROV-PINSK

Brest

Pinsk

(1252-54) Turov

CHERNIHIV

NOVHOROD-
SIVERS'KYI

Novhorod-Sivers'kyi

Kursk

VOLHYNIA

Liubech
Chernihiv

Putyvl'

Chełm
(Kholm)

(1289-
1302)

Volodymyr

Sandomierz

Cherven

Luts'k

KIEV

Kiev

Cracow

Belz

(1238-40)

PEREIASLAV

Jarosław
(Iaroslav)

L'viv

Zvenyhorod

Pereiaslav

Przemyśl
(Peremyshl')

H O R D E

Halych

Terebovlia

Košice

(1280-
1320)

GALICIA

HUNGARIAN

Buda

Pest

KINGDOM

C A R P A T H I A N   M O U N T A I N S

G O L D E N

(1160-1240) G

SEA OF
AZOV

Bilhorod

Tmutorokan

Sugdea

BLACK SEA

Approximate international boundaries

Approximate principality boundaries

Southern boundary of Lithuania
by 1263

Galicia-Volhynia

Other lands under Galicia-Volhynia

Baltic-Black Sea trade route

Other major trade routes

Present Ukrainian S.S.R. boundary

Scale 1: 6 830 000

0   50   100   150 Miles

0   50   100   150 Kilometers

MAP 9

Ukrainian lands circa 1400

By the time Galicia-Volhynia was eliminated as an independent entity during the second half of the fourteenth century, Ukrainian lands were for the most part under the control of two states: the Grand Duchy of Lithuania and the Mongolo-Tatar Golden Horde. In the far west, smaller portions of Ukrainian territory were ruled by Poland (Galicia), Hungary (Transcarpathia), and Moldavia (northern Bukovina and southern Bessarabia).

The Golden Horde, or Kipchak Khanate, as the westernmost portion of the Mongol Empire was known, had been founded in the second half of the thirteenth century by Khan Batu (d. 1254), who between 1237 and 1241 had conquered and destroyed many cities in Kievan Rus'. Despite Batu's well-deserved reputation as a fierce warrior, his Mongol successors were content with accepting tribute from the Rus' princes and were primarily interested in establishing their control over the rich trading routes that passed through their lands near the mouths of the Volga and Don rivers. Their capitals along the lower Volga (Old and New Sarai) became major stops on the caravan routes from Central Asia and China to the Black and Mediterranean seas. From Sarai, trade routes via caravan continued westward to the Mongol town of Solkhat (Staryi Krym) in the Crimea or via the Don River and Sea of Azov to the coastal cities along the Straits of Kerch and the Black Sea.

The Mongols, who realized the value of international trade, encouraged the revival of the Crimean coastal cities, this time under the leadership of Italian merchants from Venice, Pisa, and most especially Genoa, who had already been plying the Black Sea (see Map 6). Beginning in the second half of the thirteenth century, Genoese-controlled Caffa (formerly Theodosia) became the primary commercial center in a region that saw the revitalization of the old commercial centers of Bosporan Kingdom fame. Panticapaeum became Vosporo; Tanais, Tana; Tmutorokan, Matrega; Sugdea, Soldaia; and farther west the Genoese developed Cembalo (later Balaklava) and Moncastro (formerly Bilhorod). Thus, between the late thirteenth and fifteenth centuries, the age-old symbiotic relationship between the steppe hinterland and the coastal cities was re-established, bringing about an era of stability to the eastern and southern Ukraine under the hegemony of the Golden Horde and Italian traders from Venice and especially Genoa.

At about the same time that the Mongols were consolidating their rule over the lands west of the Caspian Sea, much farther north near the Baltic Sea a new political force was in the making. There, along the marshy lowlands between the Western Dvina and Nieman rivers, several heathen tribes of Lithuanians, who felt threatened by the prosletyzing expansion of the Germanic Teutonic and Livonian Christian military orders, united under the leadership of Prince Mindaugas (d. 1263). Although the Lithuanians were able to hold back the Germanic knights, their own expansive designs were checked on the Baltic; thus, they turned toward the south and east, to Rus' territories.

The descendants of Mindaugas were remarkably successful, and within one century, they were able to expand the Grand Duchy of Lithuania's territory to include all of the Rus' principalities of Polotsk, Pinsk, Turov, Volhynia, Chernihiv, Novhorod-Sivers'kyi, Kiev, much of Smolensk in the northeast, and the frontier region known as Podolia in the southwest. Before the end of the fourteenth century, the Lithuanians were even able to increase their sphere of influence as far as the Black Sea (between the mouths of the Dniester and Dnieper rivers), so that most Ukrainian lands came to be within the borders of their grand duchy.

This rapid Lithuanian advance was the result of military successes against the Poles (Podlachia, Volhynia, and Podolia were particular bones of contention) and the Golden Horde, as well as the implementation of a policy whereby the Lithuanians changed little in the Rus' territories they took over. Most Rus' princes were left to rule over their traditional patrimonies, and the laws, social structure, Orthodox religion, and Slavonic language from the Kievan Rus' era were basically left in place.

Despite its success in territorial growth, the Grand Duchy of Lithuania was frequently wracked by problems of succession, civil war, and intervention by outside powers, often at the invitation of its own rulers. The result of one such conflict was an alliance with Poland that led in 1385 to the union of the two countries through the person of their common ruler, the first of whom was the Lithuanian Jogaila/Jagiełło (reigned 1386–1434). Although the two halves of the joint kingdom remained politically and administratively distinct, Lithuania in subsequent decades was brought closer to Poland, a development which eventually was to have great significance for Ukrainian territory still within the borders of the grand duchy.

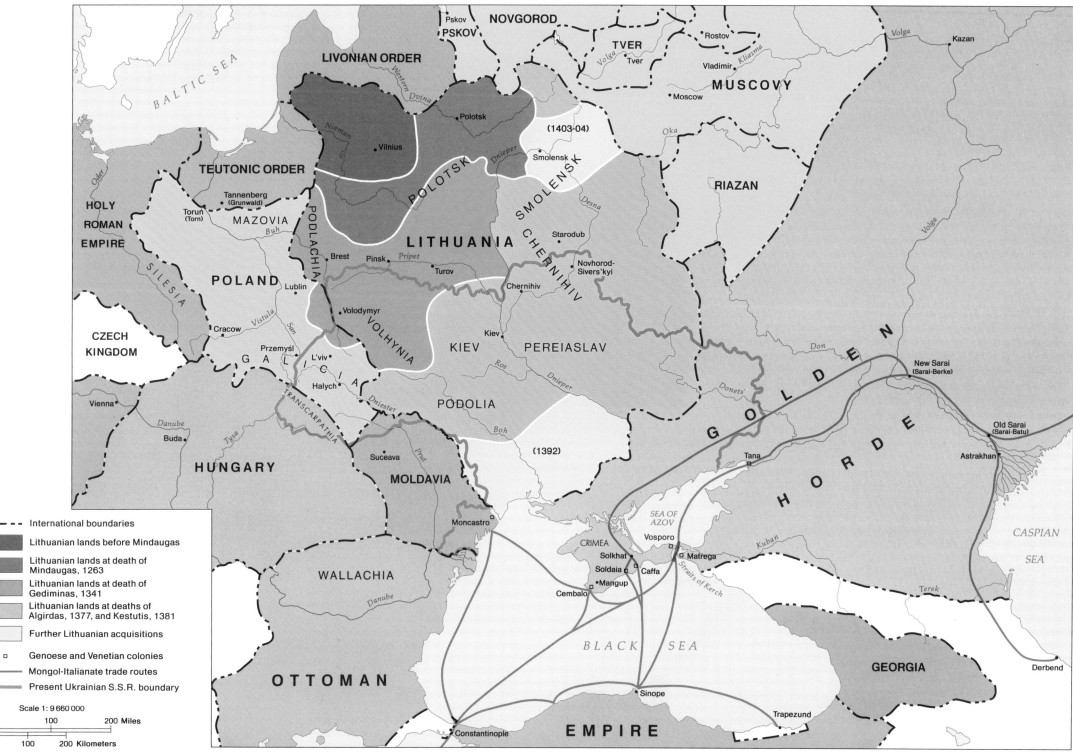

MAP 10

Ukrainian lands after 1569

The year 1569 witnessed the conclusion of several months of negotiations between Polish and Lithuanian leaders which resulted in an agreement signed at Lublin, whereby the Grand Duchy of Lithuania and the Kingdom of Poland, until then united only through the person of a common king, henceforth became the Polish-Lithuanian Commonwealth ruled by a common diet. The Union of Lublin also recognized the acquisition by Poland of Podlachia, Volhynia, Kiev, and Podolia. As a result, all Ukrainian lands that had formerly belonged to the Grand Duchy of Lithuania now formed an integral part of the Polish component in the joint commonwealth.

Administratively, these new territorial acquisitions were divided into several palatinates. Thus, to the Lublin, Chełm, Belz, and Galicia or Red Rus' (Rus' Czerwona) palatinates, which already belonged to Poland, were added the palatinates of Volhynia, Kiev, Podolia, Bratslav (formerly part of Podolia), and, after 1619, Chernihiv. It is also from the late sixteenth and early seventeenth centuries that the term Ukraine came to be used as a designation for a specific territory, which in Polish sources referred to the palatinates of Kiev, Bratslav, and Chernihiv.

The fate of Chernihiv was typical of those border areas located between Poland-Lithuania and Muscovy which were to change hands several times during the sixteenth and seventeenth centuries. After 1619, when Poland's borders reached their farthest eastward extent, a steady westward advance of Muscovy followed, which resulted in its progressive acquisition of territories in eastern Lithuania and the eastern Ukraine.

The southeastern Ukraine during this period had become the meeting-place for three spheres of influence: Polish, Muscovite, and Crimean Tatar. Actually the international boundaries between the lower Dnieper and lower Donets' rivers as marked on this map were really only symbolic, because this whole region was a kind of no-man's land dominated by nomadic and free-booting communities of Zaporozhian Cossacks and Nogay Tatars. The Cossacks of Zaporozhia (from their early center on the Dnieper island of Khortytsia; see Map 11) were ostensibly under Polish hegemony and the Nogays were supposedly subordinate to the Crimean Khanate, but both groups and the regions they inhabited were in fact self-governing and not particularly responsible to the central authority of the states who claimed to rule over them.

As for the Crimean Khanate, it had come into existence after the disintegration of the Golden Horde in the fifteenth century. By the middle of that century, the Khanate also had its own ruling dynasty, the Girays, who organized a state from their capital at Solkhat and later Bakhchesarai. Before long, however, the Crimean Khanate was to be drawn into the Ottoman sphere of influence. The expanding Ottoman Turks had by 1475 captured Caffa (renamed Kefe) and the other Genoese-dominated coastal cities placing them under their direct control. The Turkish presence also led to a situation in which the Crimean Khanate became a client state (albeit independent in its foreign policy) of the Ottoman Empire. While the Crimean rulers were content to be financially subsidized by the Ottoman Empire, they were unable or unwilling to control the several nomadic Nogay Tatar tribes who during the second half of the sixteenth century settled in and controlled the steppe region north of the Black Sea and Sea of Azov. It was the Nogays who made annual forays into the Polish Ukraine and Muscovy for slaves, who were then sold for a handsome profit by Crimean merchants. And it was this Crimean, or more precisely Nogay, Tatar threat which prompted the rise of the Zaporozhian Cossack movement which by the seventeenth century was to transform Ukrainian society.

DENMARK

BALTIC SEA

LIVONIA

COURLAND

Tver

Volga

Kliazma

TSARDOM

Moscow

Polotsk

Western *Dvina*

OF

PRUSSIA

Gdańsk

Vilnius

LITHUANIA

Oka

MUSCOVY

POLISH-

Desna

Smolensk

BRANDENBURG

Berlin

Nieman

Dnieper

Oder

MAZOVIA

LITHUANIAN

Starodub

Buh

PODLACHIA

P

Vistula

Warsaw

Pripet

O

GREAT POLAND

Brest

CHERNIHIV

L

Chernihiv

SILESIA

LITTLE POLAND

Lublin

Chełm

COMMONWEALTH

Volodymyr

A

Luts'k VOLHYNIA

Kiev

Prague

N

Pereiaslav

Lubny

Don

HABSBURG EMPIRE

Cracow

Ostrih

D

KIEV

BOHEMIA

Belz

Korsun'

Cherkasy

Przemyśl

MORAVIA

L'viv

GALICIA

Chyhyryn

Dnieper

Donets'

Halych

Dniester

PODOLIA

Kamianets'-
Podil's'kyi

Bratslav

Kodak

ZAPOROZHIA

Vienna

Danube

Tysa

Khotyn

BRATSLAV

Sich

Boh

Prut

Buda

TRANSYLVANIA

MOLDAVIA

Jassy

CRIMEAN KHANATE

Azov

Ochakiv

EMPIRE

SEA OF AZOV

Kuban

HUNGARY

O T T O M A N

Akkerman

Ievpatoriia
(Gözleve)

Solkhat

Bakhchesarai

Caffa
(Kefe)

CIRCASSIANS

WALLACHIA

Kiliia

Balaklava

Danube

BLACK SEA

Legend

- – · – International boundaries, 1569
- – – – Boundaries of semi-independent entities
- - - - - Boundaries of Polish palatinates on Ukrainian lands
- ▦ Farthest eastward extent of the Polish-Lithuanian Commonwealth, 1619
- ◉ Palatinate administrative centers
- ▓ Present Ukrainian S.S.R. boundary

Scale 1 : 8 000 000

0 — 100 — 200 Miles

0 — 100 — 200 Kilometers

10

MAP 11
Zaporozhia

The Cossacks, who by the sixteenth century were well established in the central and south-central Ukraine, evolved into two distinct groups. The 'town Cossacks' resided in and around frontier settlements like Cherkasy, Chyhyryn, and Bratslav (see Map 10), where they served the Lithuanian and later Polish authorities in defense against Tatar raids. The association with at least one frontier town, Cherkasy, remained strong, so that contemporary Muscovite and Tatar documents referred to all Cossacks, regardless of their origin, as *Cherkassy*.

The second group consisted of Cossacks who lived outside the frontier towns, along the banks of the lower Dnieper River beyond any effective control of Lithuanian or Polish authority. Because they settled south or beyond the Dnieper rapids (in Ukrainian, *za porohamy*), this second group of Cossacks came to be known as the Zaporozhian Cossacks or the Zaporozhian Host, and the territory they inhabited on both sides of the Dnieper River was called Zaporozhia.

The Zaporozhian Cossacks built their own fortified centers which, although frequently changing location, generally carried the name Sich. The Sich served as both a military camp and marketplace for goods from the Crimea and Ottoman lands in the south and from other Ukrainian and Polish lands farther north. By the seventeenth century, the Sich also served as the administrative center for the whole region of Zaporozhia.

The Sich was usually built on islands in the Dnieper River and its tributaries. The first Sich was founded on Little Khortytsia Island (Mala Khortytsia, 1552–1558), and subsequent ones generally moved progressively southward: Tomakivka (1564–1593), Bazavluk (1593–1630), Mykytyn Rih (1628–1652), and Stara Sich (1652–1709). In 1709, a Muscovite army destroyed Stara Sich and the Cossacks were forced to abandon Zaporozhia altogether; they placed themselves under Ottoman protection and built their Sich at Oleshky (1711–1734) near the mouth of the Dnieper River (see inset). In 1734, the Zaporozhians returned to their original homeland where they set up a 'new sich'—Nova Sich—which lasted until 1775, when it too was abolished and all of Zaporozhia was placed under a Russian administration responsible directly to the tsar in St. Petersburg.

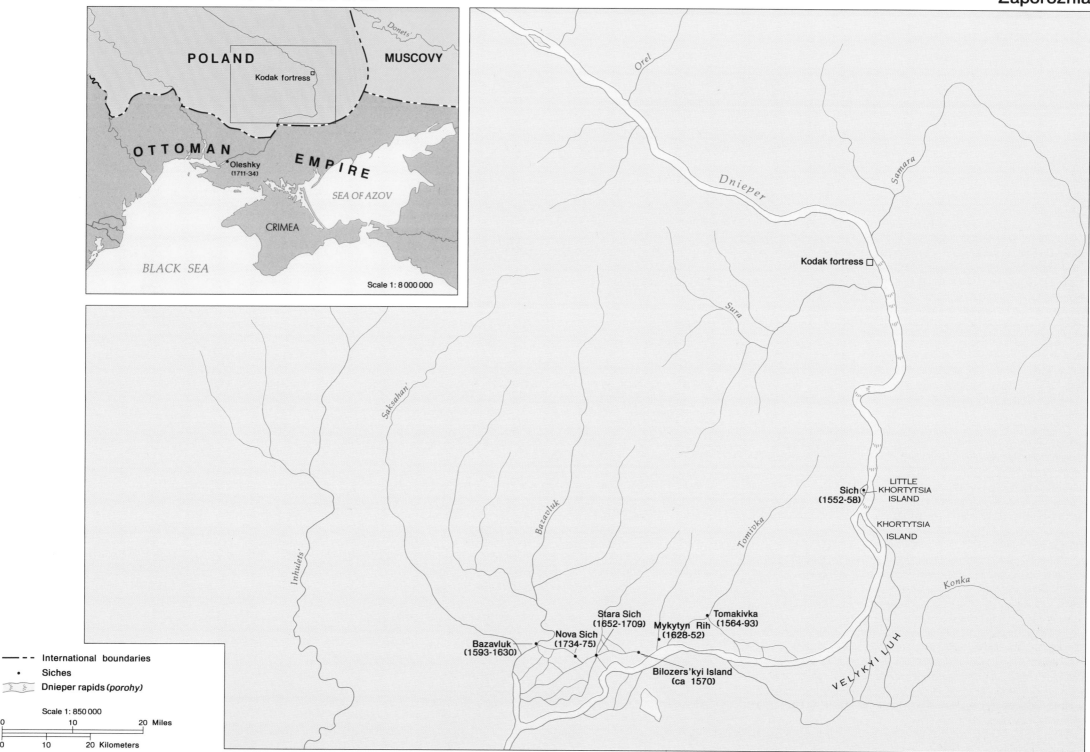

POLAND

MUSCOVY

Kodak fortress □

OTTOMAN

EMPIRE

• Oleshky
(1711-34)

SEA OF AZOV

CRIMEA

BLACK SEA

Scale 1: 8 000 000

Donets'

Orel

Dnieper

Samara

Kodak fortress □

Sura

Saksahan'

Tomivka

Bazavluk

Sich •
(1552-58)

LITTLE
KHORTYTSIA
ISLAND

KHORTYTSIA
ISLAND

Inhulets'

Konka

Stara Sich
(1652-1709)

Tomakivka
(1564-93)

Mykytyn Rih
(1628-52)

Nova Sich
(1734-75)

Bazavluk
(1593-1630)

Bilozers'kyi Island
(ca 1570)

VELYKYI LUH

- - -   International boundaries

•   Siches

Dnieper rapids *(porohy)*

Scale 1: 850 000

0   10   20 Miles

0   10   20 Kilometers

MAP 12

Ecclesiastical divisions in the sixteenth and seventeenth centuries

Ever since the Kievan period, religion in the form of Eastern Orthodox Christianity had been an integral part of East Slavic culture. Moreover, the fusion of religious and territorial/'national' identity, which had been characteristic of Kievan times, prevailed in the Lithuanian and Ukrainian Rus' lands at least until the seventeenth century. Consequently, one was of the Rus' land because one was of the Orthodox Rus' faith and vice versa.

Initially, the Orthodox churches of all the East Slavs—Ukrainians, Belorussians, and Russians—were under the jurisdiction of the ecumenical patriarch in Constantinople. However, after 1448 the Orthodox church in Muscovy chose its own metropolitan, eventually becoming autocephalous, or independent; after 1589 it was headed by its own patriarch in Moscow. The Orthodox Rus' inhabitants (Ukrainians and Belorussians) ruled by Lithuania and Poland continued to remain under the jurisdiction of the ecumenical patriarch. This jurisdiction was known as the metropolitan see of Kiev and Halych.

By the sixteenth century, the Kievan metropolitan see comprised ten dioceses (or eparchies). Seven of these—Kiev (including Vilnius), Luts'k, Volodymyr (including Brest), L'viv-Halych, Przemyśl, Chełm, and Chernihiv-Briansk—were wholly or partly on Ukrainian territories; the remaining three—Turov-Pinsk, Polotsk, and Smolensk—covered Belorussian territories. There was also an Orthodox bishopric in Transcarpathia with its seat at Mukachevo that was directly subordinate to the ecumenical patriarch in Constantinople.

With the fall of Constantinople in 1453, the Kievan metropolitanate was effectively cut off from its spiritual head. This fact, combined with the practice of Polish kings to fill vacant Orthodox bishoprics with their own political sympathizers (often from the secular nobility), led to a decline in the effectiveness and moral standards, especially at the hierarchical level, of the Kievan metropolitanate. Initially, the response of some Orthodox Rus' faithful was withdrawal, either by emigrating to Orthodox Muscovite lands, or by retreating to monasteries (among them Zhovkva, Skyt Maniavs'kyi, L'viv, Pochaïv, Zhydychyn, Dubno, Derman', Ovruch, and Kiev on Ukrainian lands), which flourished during the sixteenth century.

Another more 'worldly oriented' response was made during the second half of the sixteenth century by certain Orthodox Rus' magnates and townsmen. The magnates founded schools and printing presses on their estates like Zabłudów in Podlachia and Ostrih in Volhynia. The townsmen banded together in brotherhoods, whose intention was to improve the financial, educational, and moral standards of Orthodoxy. The most important brotherhood was founded in L'viv (1585). It served as a model for several brotherhoods in the western Ukraine set up before the end of the sixteenth century (Kamianets'-Podil's'kyi, Rohatyn, Horodok, Brest, Przemyśl, Lublin, Halych) as well as for others established in the seventeenth century (Chełm, Ostrih, Luts'k, Nemyriv, Kiev, and elsewhere).

This Orthodox cultural revival was taking place at a time when Poland itself was a fertile ground for secular and religious cultural activity associated with the impact there of the Renaissance, Reformation, and Counter-Reformation. Orthodox magnates were particularly close to Protestant thinkers and were influenced by their more rational approach and emphasis on the need for knowledge and education. Such intellectual activity also prompted discussions among the Orthodox about the problem of church unity. This issue already had a long tradition in the western Rus' lands and was now once again being raised as a possibility. The Counter-Reformation led by Jesuits in Poland also discussed church unity, but from a Roman Catholic perspective.

Theoretical discussions and practical results were, of course, two different things. In an atmosphere of much controversy, pro-union and anti-union Orthodox hierarchs and lay leaders met in separate councils in the city of Brest, where in 1596 the pro-union council proclaimed the union of the Kievan metropolitanate with Rome. The resulting Uniate (later known as Greek Catholic and today Ukrainian Catholic) church was to retain its traditional eastern rite and privileges, but to recognize as its head the pope in Rome instead of the ecumenical patriarch in Constantinople. Not all bishops accepted the union, however, so that the seventeenth century witnessed a particularly complicated and often confusing overlap of ecclesiastical jurisdictions. There often existed two metropolitans—Orthodox and Uniate—each claiming authority over the

whole Kievan metropolitanate; two new dioceses—Brest and Vilnius—came into being; and other dioceses were either Orthodox or Uniate, or they had simultaneously two bishops in conflict with each other for control of the faithful and of diocesan property. Immediately after 1596, Orthodoxy was outlawed, and although legalized again after 1607, the Polish government generally favored the Uniate bishops and did not recognize any newly chosen Orthodox hierarchs until 1632.

In neighboring Transcarpathia, the movement for church union culminated in 1646 with the Union of Uzhhorod. A rival Orthodox diocese continued to function for several decades in the far eastern part of the region, while the new Uniate diocese with its seat in Mukachevo remained subordinate to the Roman Catholic Hungarian diocese of Eger until it gained full independent episcopal status during the second half of the eighteenth century. In Bukovina, meanwhile, the Ukrainian populace remained Orthodox under the jurisdiction of the metropolitanate of Moldavia with its seat in Suceava and after 1630 in Jassy.

As for the initiators of the late sixteenth-century Orthodox cultural revival, the magnates, many of them and especially their offspring converted to Roman Catholicism. Only the brotherhoods and certain monasteries remained staunch defenders of Orthodoxy. But in the context of Roman Catholic Polish society, these Orthodox groups needed help from an entity with more political and military influence. They found that help in the Zaporozhian Cossacks on the southeastern steppes, who by the first half of the seventeenth century had proclaimed themselves ready to act in whatever way necessary to defend the best interests of Orthodoxy.

SWEDEN

DENMARK

BALTIC SEA

COURLAND

LIVONIA

Western

Dvina

Psrov

TSARDOM

Tver

Iaroslavl'

Suzdal'

OF

Moskva

Volga

Moscow

Oka

Gdańsk

PRUSSIA

Nieman

Vilnius

LITHUANIA

Polotsk

Smolensk

Riazan'

BRANDENBURG

Berlin

Oder

P

Vistula

Buh

O

Mahiloŭ
(Mogilev)

Mstislav

Minsk

Dnieper

Zabłudów

Slutsk

Briansk

Starodub

MUSCOVY

Don

Warsaw

L

Brest

Pinsk

Pripet

Turov

Desna

Chernihiv

Prague

HABSBURG

Lublin

A

Chełm

Volodymyr

Zhydychyn

Luts'k

Dubno

N

Derman'

D

Ovruch

Kiev

Cracow

San

EMPIRE

Przemysl

Zhovkva

L'viv

Horodok

Univ

Rohatyn

Pochaïv

Ostrih

Ternopil'

Dnieper

Vienna

Danube

Eger

Halych

Dniester

Skyt
Maniavs'kyi

Nemyriv

Kamianets'-
Podil's'kyi

Boh

ZAPOROZHIA

Don

Donets'

Mukachevo

Tysa

TRANSYLVANIA

Prut

Suceava

MOLDAVIA

Jassy

CRIMEAN KHANATE

SEA OF AZOV

HUNGARY

OTTOMAN

EMPIRE

Kuban

WALLACHIA

Danube

Caffa

Bakhchesarai

CIRCASSIANS

BLACK SEA

International boundaries after 1569

Boundaries of semi-independent
entities after 1569

Boundaries of Orthodox or Uniate
dioceses

Farthest eastward extent of the Polish-
Lithuanian Commonwealth, 1619

Orthodox or Uniate dioceses

Important monasteries

Present Ukrainian S.S.R. boundary

Scale 1: 8 000 000

0   100   200 Miles

0   100   200 Kilometers

12

MAP 13

The Cossack state after 1649

While the first half of the seventeenth century witnessed a new low point in the history of Orthodoxy on Ukrainian lands, it also saw the growing strength of the Zaporozhian Cossack movement. By the outset of the century, the Cossacks had distinguished themselves in raids against several cities of the Ottoman Empire, both north and south of the Black Sea, as well as in the service of Poland in its campaigns against Muscovy. Besides their self-confident military exploits, the Zaporozhians also began, during the 1620s, to proclaim themselves as defenders of the Orthodox Rus' people of Ukraine. Cossack military strength, combined with an ideological justification to defend Orthodoxy, was bound to bring them into conflict with the state under whose ostensible authority they lived—Poland. Not surprisingly, many revolts and battles took place between the Polish army and recalcitrant Cossacks during the 1620s and 1630s.

This growing heritage of Polish-Cossack friction culminated in 1648 in the outbreak of a new revolt, led by a Cossack hetman named Bohdan Khmel'nyts'kyi (1595–1657). The surprisingly rapid Cossack victories during 1648 in several battles against the Poles (Zhovti Vody, Korsun', Pyliavtsi) brought Khmel'nyts'kyi's forces by November as far west as Zamość (Zamostia) and at the same time transformed the revolt into a social and political revolution. Although Khmel'nyts'kyi himself had never intended to separate Cossack lands from Poland, the revolutionary events forced him to reassess his goals. Having brought a significant portion of the Ukraine under his control, the Cossack leader began to create an administrative structure for the territory.

The Cossack state actually came into existence following an armistice reached at the town of Zboriv in August 1649 between Khmel'nyts'kyi and the Polish government. Known officially as the Army of Zaporozhia or Zaporozhian Host, the new Cossack state comprised the former Polish palatinates of Kiev (including Zaporozhia), Bratslav, and Chernihiv (together with the region around Starodub). These three palatinates—until then together called Ukraine—were to be cleared of Polish administrative and military authorities, who were to be replaced by Cossacks. Although Zaporozhia recognized the suzerainty of Hetman Khmel'nyts'kyi, the region from the outset did not have the same administrative structure as the rest of the Cossack state and in later years it became a distinct political entity.

As its name implies, the Army of Zaporozhia, or the Cossack state, was organized along military lines. With the exception of Zaporozhia, the state was divided into military/administrative units called regimental districts (*polky*), which in turn were each subdivided into companies (*sotni*). The number of these regimental districts varied, depending on political circumstances and the state's fluctuating borders. There were at least twenty regiments that maintained a certain stability and many others that lasted for only a few years. In late 1649, just after the establishment of the Cossack state, there were 16 regimental districts (indicated on accompanying Map 13) with a total of 272 companies. In the course of the next two decades, several other regiments were founded, although they lasted for only a short interval; four others were created or re-established – Pavoloch, Lubny, Starodub, Hadiach – and these existed for a significant length of time. The first capital of the Cossack state was Chyhyryn, a town near Khmel'nyts'kyi's estate.

With regard to Zaporozhia, the Cossack elders there had initially recognized Hetman Khmel'nyts'kyi as their leader, although even before his death in 1657, the Zaporozhians had begun to follow their own autonomous orientation. After 1686, their territory was officially designated the Army of Lower Zaporozhia, in order to distinguish it from the rest of the Cossack state (the Army of Zaporozhia). Lower Zaporozhian territory was divided into 38 units (*kureni*) and was ruled by a leader elected annually known as the *koshovyi otaman*. This leader together with a small staff of officials resided in an administrative center called the Sich (see Map 11).

PRUSSIA

MAZOVIA

PODLACHIA

LITHUANIA

• Mahiloŭ

• Chausy

BELGOROD LINE

POLISH-LITHUANIAN

• Warsaw

• Brest

Buh

Pripet

• Starodub

CHERNIHIV

MUSCOVY

• Voronezh

LUBLIN

• Chełm

SANDOMIERZ

Vistula

VOLHYNIA

COMMONWEALTH

• Zamość

San

Chernihiv •

• Ovruch

Nizhyn

Putyvl'

Konotop ✕
(July 8, 1659)

Seim

SLOBODA

Don

• Belgorod

BELZ

✕ Berestechko
(June 1651)

Kiev •

Pryluky •

Hadiach •

Okhtyrka •

UKRAINE

GALICIA

(RUS')

• L'viv

✕ Zboriv
(Aug 1649)

✕ Pyliavtsi
(Sept 1648)

PODOLIA

Pavoloch •

Bila Tserkva •

KIEV

Kaniv •

Pereiaslav •

Kropyvna •

Lubny •

Myrhorod •

Cherkasy •

Poltava •

Vorskla

Donets'

• Vinnytsia

✕ Zhvanets'
(Sept-Nov 1653)

Kal'nyk •

Dryzhypole ✕
(Jan-Feb 1655)

Korsun ✕
(May 15-16,
1648)

Chyhyryn •

Dnieper

Uman' •

Bratslav •

BRATSLAV

✕ Batih
(June 1652)

Kodak •

ZAPOROZHIA

Zhovti Vody ✕
(May 5-6, 1648)

TRANSYLVANIA

MOLDAVIA

• Jassy

Stara Sich •

Prut

Dniester

Buh

Tysa

OTTOMAN

EMPIRE

Dnieper

CRIMEAN KHANATE

SEA OF AZOV

Don

Kuban

WALLACHIA

• Bakhchesarai

CIRCASSIANS

Danube

BLACK SEA

---------- International boundaries, 1648

------ Boundaries of semi-independent
entities, 1648

------ Palatinate boundaries

▨ Cossack State, 1649

▨ Areas briefly under Cossack control

·········· Cossack regimental district
boundaries

⊙ Regimental district centers,
October, 1649

✕ Major battles of Khmel'nyts'kyi era

⇐ Khmel'nyts'kyi's 1648 campaign

ᴗᴗᴗᴗ Muscovite anti-Tatar defense line

▬▬ Present Ukrainian S.S.R. boundary

Scale 1: 5 580 000

0   50   100   150 Miles

0   50   100   150   Kilometers

13

MAP 14

Ukrainian lands after 1667

Despite the creation of a Cossack state in 1649, the struggle against the Poles continued. By 1653, the military conflict had reached a stalemate, in which neither side was able to score a definitive victory. From the beginning of the revolution in 1648, Khmel'nyts'kyi had sought alliances with several neighboring powers (Ottoman Empire, Moldavia, Transylvania, Muscovy), and finally in 1654 he reached an agreement at Pereiaslav with Muscovy. As a result of the Pereiaslav agreement, the Cossack state came under the protection of the tsar, who added to his title Little Russia, the term used in official Muscovite/Russian sources to describe the newly acquired territory.

The immediate result of Pereiaslav was war between Muscovy, which now had the aid of the Cossacks, and Poland, which became allied with Muscovy's enemy, the Tatars. The longer-term result of Pereiaslav was that it plunged Ukrainian territories (as well as much of Poland-Lithuania) into thirty-two years of almost unending foreign invasion, civil war, and social upheaval, during which the human and physical resources of the country were devastated. In the course of this period, known as the *Ruïna* (Ruin or Deluge), Cossack leaders who succeeded Khmel'nyts'kyi (d. 1657) tried to maintain the independent or at least autonomous status of their state by aligning with one of the warring powers—whether Poland, Muscovy, the Ottoman Empire—or the enemies of those powers—Sweden in the far north and Transylvania to the southwest. At times there were separate Cossack governments led by hetmans on the Right Bank and Left Bank. The old Cossack capital of Chyhyryn (1649–1663 and for the Right Bank only, 1665–1676) was transferred to Hadiach (1663–1669) and then to Baturyn (1669–1708).

In the end, the Cossacks were unable to obtain independence, and the state Khmel'nyts'kyi had created was divided between Poland, Muscovy, and the Ottoman Empire. For several decades (1672–1699), the Ottomans controlled the palatinates of Podolia, Bratslav, and southern Kiev almost as far north as the city of Kiev, but subsequently they were pushed back into their traditional sphere along the Black Sea coast and Crimea. As for Poland and Muscovy, the Dnieper River became, after a treaty signed at Andrusovo in 1667, the new dividing line between those two competing powers. Thus, the Left Bank Ukraine, including Kiev and the surrounding region as well as Zaporozhia on both sides of the Dnieper, became part of Muscovy; the Right Bank Ukraine remained under Poland.

Despite the signing of an 'eternal peace' in 1686 between Poland and Muscovy reaffirming their respective spheres of influence in Ukraine, wars were to continue and borders were to change, especially during the rule of the dynamic Cossack hetman Ivan Mazepa (in office 1687–1709) and the first phase of the Great Northern War involving Muscovy, Sweden, and Poland, which culminated in the victory of Muscovy over Sweden and its allies (including Hetman Mazepa) at the Battle of Poltava in June 1709. Nonetheless, the basic division of Ukrainian territory between Poland, Muscovy, and the Ottoman Empire, such as it had become established by the end of the seventeenth century, was to remain in place until the second half of the eighteenth century. As for the Cossacks, it was only within the Muscovite sphere that they maintained a degree of territorial autonomy and this varied in the three regions they inhabited: the Hetmanate, Zaporozhia, and the Sloboda Ukraine.

BRANDENBURG/
PRUSSIA

LITHUANIA

• Andrusovo

MUSCOVY

MAZOVIA

PODLACHIA

Buh

• Warsaw

POLISH - LITHUANIAN

Pripet

Starodub •

BELGOROD LINE

• Voronezh

LUBLIN

Chełm •

VOLHYNIA

Chernihiv •

HETMANATE

Putyvl' •

Seim

SANDOMIERZ

Vistula

BELZ

COMMONWEALTH

Nizhyn •

Baturyn •

Don

SLOBODA

Kiev •

Hadiach •

Belgorod •

Przemyśl •

GALICIA

L'viv •

KIEV

Pereiaslav •

Lubny •

Okhtyrka •

San

(RUS')

Bila Tserkva •

Poltava •

IZIUM LINE

UKRAINE

HABSBURG
EMPIRE

PODOLIA

Cherkasy •

Vorskla

Izium •

Donets'

Kamianets'-
Podil's'kyi •

Bratslav •

Uman' •

Chyhyryn •

Mukachevo •

BRATSLAV

Donets

Dnieper

Tysa

ZAPOROZHIA

TRANSYLVANIA

Prut

Dniester

Kodak •

MOLDAVIA

Stara Sich •

Boh

Don

Azov •

Ochakiv •

Dnieper

CRIMEAN KHANATE

OTTOMAN EMPIRE

SEA OF AZOV

International boundaries, 1667

Boundaries of semi-independent
entities

Palatinate boundaries

Under Ottoman control, 1672–99

Muscovite anti-Tatar defense lines

Present Ukrainian S.S.R. boundary

Scale 1: 5 580 000

0   50   100   150 Miles

0   50   100   150 Kilometers

WALLACHIA

Bakhchesarai •

Kuban

CIRCASSIANS

BLACK SEA

Danube

14

MAP 15

Ukrainian lands circa 1750

The eighteenth century witnessed two interrelated developments of direct significance for Ukraine: (1) the westward and southward expansion of the Russian Empire which brought most Ukrainian lands under its control; and (2) the progressive dissolution of the autonomy enjoyed by the three Cossack entities: the Hetmanate, Zaporozhia, and the Sloboda Ukraine. Both developments were in particular evidence during the reign of Empress Catherine II (1762–1796).

The first of the Cossack entities to lose its autonomous status was the Sloboda Ukraine. It had come into existence during the seventeenth century when refugees from the Polish-Cossack wars sought refuge by going eastward to Muscovy. There, along the tsar's southern frontier, they were allowed to establish free settlements, or *slobody*, from which the region derived its name. Muscovy had encouraged such settlement, which together with its own fortified defense system—the Belgorod Line (1630s–1640s) and Izium Line (1670s), see Maps 13 and 14—helped to protect territories farther north from Tatar incursions. Although a Cossack military/administrative system was set up (with five regiments after 1685 based in Sumy, Okhtyrka, Kharkiv, Izium, and Ostrogozhsk), the Sloboda Ukraine had never been part of the Cossack state; it was, however, allowed a wide degree of local autonomy under the direct authority of the central Muscovite/Russian government. As part of its process of internal integration, in 1765 the Russian government abolished the five Sloboda Cossack regiments and transformed the whole territory into an imperial province (called Sloboda Ukraine) responsible directly to the central tsarist administration in St. Petersburg.

Farther south, Zaporozhia experienced an even more turbulent history and accompanying administrative change. The old Army of Lower Zaporozhia (as the territory was officially known) ceased to exist at the outset of the eighteenth century, following the Zaporozhian alliance with Hetman Mazepa and the Swedes during the latter's invasion of Muscovy. Reacting to that alliance, in 1709 Tsar Peter I (reigned 1682–1725) ordered the destruction of the Stara Sich, forcing most Zaporozhians to flee to the Ottoman Empire, where they set up a new center at Oleshky near the mouth of the Dnieper River.

In 1734, the Russian government allowed several thousand Zaporozhian Cossacks to return to their homeland and to govern themselves in an autonomous entity known as the Free Lands of the Zaporozhian Host (Vol'nosti Viis'ka Zaporiz'koho Nyzovoho). A new or Nova Sich was established and all of Zaporozhia was divided into eight districts (*palanky*), each headed by a colonel responsible directly to the sich. But Zaporozhian autonomy was not to last long, and the Russian government soon made plans to incorporate that region into the empire as well. The first stage was to reinforce the northern frontiers of Zaporozhia by inviting settlers from abroad and other parts of the empire to settle there. As a result, three new administrative entities came into being during the 1750s: New Serbia and Slavic Serbia settled by Serbian and other Balkan immigrants, and the Sloboda regiment settled by former residents of the Sloboda Ukraine. Then, in 1775, in the wake of its successful war against the Ottoman Empire, a Russian army destroyed the Zaporozhian center at Nova Sich, forcing thousands of Cossacks to flee southwestward once again into Turkish territory beyond the Danube. All of Zaporozhia as well as the three recently established administrative entities (New Serbia, Slavic Serbia, and the Sloboda Regiment) were made part of an imperial province known as New Russia.

The process of integrating into the empire the semi-autonomous Hetmanate—officially known as Little Russia (*Malorossia*)—took several more years. The office of the hetman based in the new capital of Hlukhiv (1708–1783) was left vacant for several periods and in 1764 it was abolished altogether. A decade later, the territory of the Hetmanate was reduced, when in 1775 the southern part of the Myrhorod regiment and all of the Poltava regiment were detached and made part of the imperial province of New Russia. Finally, between 1781 and 1783, the regimental system of administration and cossack military formations were abolished. The Hetmanate ceased to exist. Its territory was subdivided into three imperial provinces—Kiev, Chernihiv, Novhorod-Sivers'kyi—which in 1796 were reunited (minus the city of Kiev and surrounding area on the Right Bank) into the Little Russian province.

Having completed the process of integrating the Sloboda Ukraine, Zaporozhia, and the Hetmanate, Empress Catherine's government was able to turn to Ukrainian territories beyond its borders. As a result of its defeat of the Ottoman Empire in 1774, Russia had acquired a small slice of territory between the mouths of the lower Boh and Dnieper rivers. The Russian-Ottoman peace treaty signed at Küçük Kainarji in 1774 also granted independence to the Crimea. That independence was short-lived, however, because in 1783 Russia annexed the peninsula and the area north and east of the Sea of Azov. Then, after defeating the Ottomans once again, in 1791 Russia obtained more territory between the lower Dniester and Boh rivers, which together with territory north of the Crimean peninsula and Sea of Azov became part of the province of New Russia. Having finally established a solid foothold in the Crimea and in land north of the Black Sea, Catherine II's administration, led by minister Grigorii Potemkin, invited immigrants (especially Germans) to New Russia, and several new cities were established, in particular the Black Sea port of Odessa.

With regard to Ukrainian lands ruled by Poland, some of the old Right Bank regimental districts from the Cossack state (see Map 13) were revived for a time by Polish authorities, once they had reacquired the region in 1699 from the Ottoman Empire. However, after 1771, the old administrative system based on the palatinates of Kiev, Podolia, and Bratslav was re-established, and the Right Bank was resettled once again by Polish landlords and peasants from the western regions of Ukraine and Poland proper. However, social instability and religious discontent continued on the Right Bank, marked especially by the so-called Haidamak revolts of 1734, 1750, and most especially 1768.

Even more serious for Poland than its internal problems were the expansionist tendencies of its neighbors: Russia, Prussia, and Austria. In 1772, these powers carried out the first territorial partition of Poland, whereby the Ukrainian-inhabited palatinates of Red Rus' (Galicia), Belz, and part of Podolia west of the Zbruch River were incorporated into Austria and made part of a new province called Galicia. Three years later, in 1775, Austria acquired

(continued)

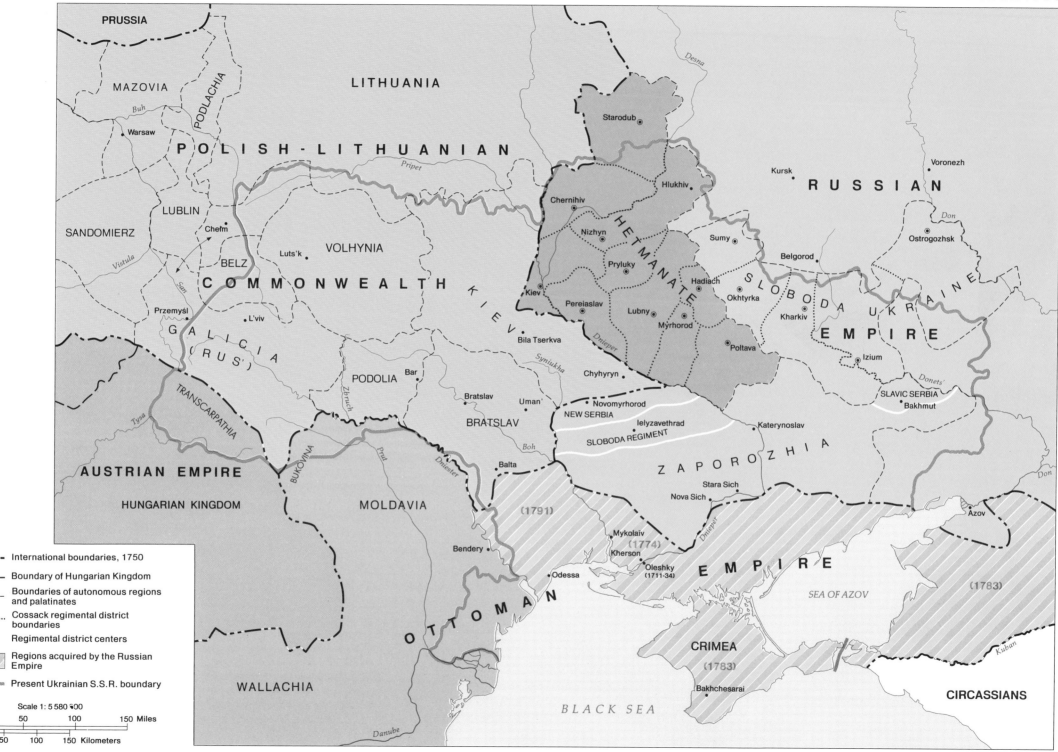

International boundaries, 1750

Boundary of Hungarian Kingdom

Boundaries of autonomous regions
and palatinates

Cossack regimental district
boundaries

Regimental district centers

Regions acquired by the Russian
Empire

Present Ukrainian S.S.R. boundary

Scale 1: 5 580 000

0   50   100   150 Miles

0   50   100   150 Kilometers

(map 15 continued)

MAP 16

The Russian Empire in Europe

from the Ottoman Empire the neighboring region of Bukovina.

Finally, in 1793 and 1795 Russia, Prussia, and Austria carried out further partitions which eliminated Poland from the map of Europe. Russia obtained the Ukrainian-inhabited palatinates of Kiev, Bratslav, Podolia, and Volhynia, and Austria received the Chełm region of the former Galician Rus' palatinate (see Map 16). Thus, by the end of the eighteenth century, all Ukrainian territories were to be found within the boundaries of two multinational empires: Russia and Austria.

Throughout the nineteenth century and the first decade and a half of the twentieth century until the outbreak of World War I in 1914, the political status of the Ukrainian lands remained basically unchanged. Those lands were ruled by two multinational states: the Russian Empire and the Austro-Hungarian Empire (see also Map 19).

The westward and southern expansion of the Russian Empire that began during the late eighteenth century with the partitions of Poland and with territorial acquisitions along the Black Sea coast from the Ottoman Empire continued during the nineteenth century. In 1809 Russia acquired Finland from Sweden; in 1812, Bessarabia from the Ottoman Empire; and in 1815, the Congress Kingdom of Poland. The first half of the nineteenth century saw further territorial acquisitions from the Ottoman Empire and Persia in the Caucasus region between the Black Sea and Caspian Sea. The earlier acquisitions from Poland and the Ottoman Empire increased Russian rule over Ukrainian territory substantially. Consequently, by 1815, as much as 85 per cent of all Ukrainian ethnolinguistic territory was in the Dnieper Ukraine, that is, within the Russian Empire.

The administrative pattern established to rule the Russian Empire's vast territory was set during the reign of Catherine II (1762–1796). In 1775 she issued the Fundamental Law for the reorganization of the state. Its goal was to divide the whole Russian Empire into imperial provinces (*namestnichestva*), each of which should have an equal number of inhabitants—about 700,000. The imperial provinces were subdivided into counties or districts (*uezdy*), which in turn comprised rural villages and cities. All of the imperial provinces had the same administrative structure headed by a governor who was appointed by and responsible directly to the tsar.

During the first decades of the nineteenth century, the imperial provinces were gradually replaced by smaller-sized provinces (*guberniia*), although they retained the same basic structure as the older units. Some provinces, most especially those located in the borderland regions, were grouped together and headed by a governor-general whose task was to co-ordinate policy over the provinces within his jurisdiction. At various times before World War I, the Ukrainian provinces had as many as three governors-general.

SWEDEN

WHITE SEA

Gulf of Bothnia

ULEÅBORG

ARKHANGELSK

TOBOLSK

VASA

KUOPIO

FINLAND

(1809)

OLONETS

VOLOGDA

ÅBO

TAVASTEHUS

ST. MICHAEL

NYLAND

VYBORG

RUSSIAN

PERM

St. Petersburg

DENMARK

ESTONIA

ST. PETERSBURG

NOVGOROD

IAROSLAVL

KOSTROMA

VIATKA

LIVONIA

BALTIC SEA

COURLAND

PSKOV

TVER

KAZAN

UFA

NETH.

KOVNO

VITEBSK

1772

Moscow

VLADIMIR

NIZHNII NOVGOROD

ORENBURG

AKMOLINSK

GERMAN EMPIRE

VILNA

1795

SMOLENSK

Moscow

KALUGA

RIAZAN

SIMBIRSK

PŁOCK

SUWAŁKI

ŁOMŻA

GRODNO

MINSK

MOGILEV

TULA

E M P I R E

KALISZ

WARSAW

POLAND

1815

SIEDLCE

1793

OREL

TAMBOV

PENZA

SAMARA

PIOTRKÓW

RADOM

CHERNIHIV

KURSK

SARATOV

KIELCE

LUBLIN

VOLHYNIA

1793

KIEV

VORONEZH

TURGAI

L'viv

Kiev

KIEV

POLTAVA

KHARKIV

DON COSSACK LANDS

URALSK

1801-55

AUSTRO-HUNGARIAN

PODOLIA

KATERYNOSLAV

ASTRAKHAN

ARAL SEA

EMPIRE

1791

KHERSON

BESSARABIA

1774

1783

SEA OF AZOV

1793

HUNGARIAN KINGDOM

1812

TAURIDA

KUBAN

STAVROPOL

SYR DARIA

1829-56

1853/85

ROMANIA

BLACK SEA

TEREK

TRANSCASPIAN REGION

SERBIA

BULGARIA

1801-64

CASPIAN SEA

KUTAIS

DAGESTAN

MONTENEGRO

1804

TIFLIS

Constantinople

BAKU

IELYZAVETPOL

1878

GREECE

OTTOMAN EMPIRE

KARS

ERIVAN

PERSIA

Legend

- ─ ·· ─ International boundaries, 1880
- ─ ─ ─ Boundaries of semi-independent entities
- ------ Province (*guberniia*) boundaries

Territorial acquisitions from the late 18th century:

- from Sweden
- from Poland
- from the Ottoman Empire
- from others
- Occupied by the Russian Empire, 1809–15
- Present Ukrainian S.S.R. boundary

Scale 1: 14 930 000

0   200   400 Miles

0   200   400 Kilometers

MAP 17

The Dnieper Ukraine, 1850

The administrative structure established throughout the Russian Empire was applied to the Dnieper Ukraine as well. At the outset of the nineteenth century, most of the imperial provinces (*namestnichestva/namisnytstva*) were replaced by the smaller-sized provinces (*guberniia*).

In 1802, in the territory of the old Hetmanate, the Little Russian province that had recently been formed was divided into the provinces of Chernihiv and Poltava. That same year, the imperial province of New Russia—created in the late eighteenth century from Zaporozhia and from lands acquired from the Ottoman Empire (see Map 16)—was divided into three provinces: Katerynoslav, Kherson, and Taurida. In the former Sloboda Ukraine, the imperial province of the same name became, in 1835, Kharkiv province (minus some territory in the north and northeast that was ceded to the Kursk and Voronezh provinces).

As for lands acquired from Poland in 1793 and 1795, these were referred to as the Southwestern Land (*Iugozapadnyi Krai*) and were divided into three provinces: Volhynia (former Volhynia and parts of Chełm and Belz palatinates), Kiev (former Kiev palatinate as well as the city and surrounding area from the Hetmanate), and Podolia (former Podolia and Bratslav palatinates). Therefore, the core Ukrainian lands in the Russian Empire consisted of nine provinces: Chernihiv, Poltava, and Kharkiv on the Left Bank; Kherson, Katerynoslav, and Taurida in the Steppe Ukraine; and Volhynia, Kiev, and Podolia on the Right Bank.

Besides these nine 'Ukrainian' provinces, there were other Ukrainian-inhabited territories within the Russian Empire. These included: (1) in the east, parts of the Kursk and Voronezh provinces, the Don Cossack Lands, and the Black Sea Cossack Lands (later Kuban province); (2) in the southwest, parts of Bessarabia province (both the region around Khotyn in the far north and the Black Sea coastal region between Odessa and the mouth of the Danube River); and (3) in the northwest, parts of the provinces of Grodno and Minsk and the eastern fringe of the Congress Kingdom of Poland. In 1861, when the Congress Kingdom effectively ceased to exist and was divided into provinces, the Ukrainian-inhabited regions there became part of the provinces of Siedlce and Lublin. Finally, in 1913, the easternmost, mainly Ukrainian-inhabited areas of those two provinces were made into the separate province of Kholm/Chełm (see Map 21).

Because the Ukrainian lands were among the borderland regions of the Russian Empire, several of the provinces were grouped together and placed under the jurisdiction of a governor-general. At certain times, there were three such posts, two of whch carried the title governor-general of Little Russia. By the 1830s, there was a Little Russian governor-general for the Right Bank (Kiev/Podolia/Volhynia, 1831–1917), a Little Russian governor-general for the Left Bank (Kharkiv/Poltava/Chernihiv, 1835–1860s), and a governor-general for New Russia (Kherson/Katerynoslav/Taurida, 1797–1874).

The provinces themselves were divided into counties (*uezdy/povity*), which in turn were subdivided into cities and villages. Some of the cities which had enjoyed the self-governing rights of Magdeburg Law from earlier centuries initially continued to administer themselves, but in 1831 they became subordinate to the provinces in which they were located. Only Kiev was temporarily unaffected by the new decree, but it too lost its self-governing privileges in 1835. However, the newer cities of Odessa and Mykolaïv along the Black Sea coast were excluded from the provincial administration and, instead, were dependent directly on the central government. With regard to the villages, they were subordinate directly to their respective counties until 1861, after which they were grouped into several rural districts (*volosti*), which in turn were subordinate to the county level.

PRUSSIA

KOVNO

VITEBSK

SMOLENSK

MOSCOW

NIZHNII
NOVGOROD

Vilnius

VILNA

Smolensk

RIAZAN

PENZA

Minsk

MOGILEV

KALUGA

TULA

PŁOCK

ŁOMŻA

GRODNO

MINSK

R U S S I A N

 OREL

TAMBOV

WARSAW

Buh

KALISZ

Warsaw

CONGRESS KINGDOM

SIEDLCE

Brest

Pinsk

CHERNIHIV

Kursk

Voronezh

SARATOV

PIOTRKÓW

OF

Chernihiv

Desna

Seim

KURSK

POLAND

RADOM

Lublin

KIELCE

LUBLIN

Chełm

VOLHYNIA

Zhytomyr

Kiev

Kharkiv

VORONEZH

Cracow

Vistula

San

G A L I C I A

L'viv

Przemyśl

Zhytomyr

KIEV

Dnieper

POLTAVA

Poltava

KHARKIV

DON

Don

AUSTRIAN

E   M   P   I   R   E

Donets

COSSACK

Uzhhorod

TRANSCARPATHIA

Kamianets'-
Podil's'kyi

PODOLIA

Katerynoslav

Danube

Tysa

Khotyn

Dniester

Ielysavethrad

KATERYNOSLAV

Buda

Pest

BUKOVINA

Balta

Kryvyi Rih

Taganrog

Rostov

EMPIRE

Boh

KHERSON

Mariiupil'

LANDS

HUNGARIAN

MOLDAVIA

BESSARABIA

Prut

Mykolaïv

KINGDOM

Kherson

BLACK SEA

Odessa

TAURIDA

SEA OF AZOV

COSSACK

LANDS

Kuban

CRIMEA

STAVROPOL

WALLACHIA

Symferopil'

BLACK SEA

CIRCASSIANS

OTTOMAN

Danube

BLACK SEA

EMPIRE

Legend:

International boundaries, 1850

Boundaries of semi-autonomous
kingdoms

Province (guberniia) boundaries

Farthest extent of Ukrainian
ethnolinguistic boundary

Present Ukrainian S.S.R. boundary

Scale 1: 6 830 000

0   50   100   150 Miles

0   50   100   150 Kilometers

MAP 18

Minority populations in nineteenth-century Ukraine

Ukrainian territories in both the Russian and Austro-Hungarian empires included by the nineteenth century many peoples who were not of Ukrainian ethnolinguistic background. According to the first general census of the Russian Empire taken in 1897, the nine 'Ukrainian' provinces contained 23,430,000 inhabitants. Of these, ethnic Ukrainians numbered slightly over 17,000,000, or 73 per cent of the population, while minority populations totalled as many as 6,000,000, or 27 per cent. The largest of the minority populations in the Dnieper Ukraine were Russians, Jews, Poles, Germans, and Tatars.

TABLE I
Ethnic Composition of the Dnieper Ukraine, 1897

Group	Number	Percentage
Ukrainians	17,000,000	72.5
Russians	2,740,000	11.7
Jews	1,927,000	8.2
Poles	656,000	2.8
Germans	515,000	2.2
Tatars	194,000	0.8
Others	398,000	1.7
TOTAL	23,430,000	

As for the Dnieper Ukraine as a whole, ethnic Ukrainians tended to live in the countryside and minority populations in urban areas. Thus, in 1897, as high as 70 per cent of the Dnieper Ukraine's urban dwellers were ethnically non-Ukrainian.

Russians began settling in the Dnieper Ukraine in the second half of the seventeenth century, when the Left Bank came under Muscovite rule. They did not come in large numbers, however, until the nineteenth century, first to the newly acquired steppe lands of New Russia (Kherson and southern Katerynoslav provinces) and the Crimea (Taurida province). After the industrialization of the Donbas region in the 1880s, Russians flocked to the mines and factories in the Donets' River valley (Kharkiv and northern Katerynoslav provinces). By 1897, 38 per cent of all Russians were urban dwellers.

Numerically, the second largest minority population in the Dnieper Ukraine comprised Jews. The Jews started coming to the Dnieper

Ukraine when the region was still part of the Polish Kingdom in the late sixteenth century. Despite several upheavals (the Khmel'nyts'kyi revolution in the seventeenth century and the Haidamak revolts in the eighteenth century) which cost many Jewish lives, their numbers continued to increase. This was particularly so in the nineteenth century. In 1850 there were about 900,000 Jews in the Dnieper Ukraine; by 1897 their numbers had more than doubled to 1,927,000. Even more so than Russians, Jews tended to live in towns and cities, which were located west of a line known as the Pale of Settlement. The Pale consisted of former lands of the Polish-Lithuanian Commonwealth beyond which Jews were forbidden to reside. Over 70 per cent of Jews inhabited places with more than 1,000 inhabitants; 26 per cent lived in twenty cities. Geographically, the Jews were concentrated in greater numbers on the Right Bank, where 61 per cent of all of them lived, averaging 12.6 per cent of the population in each of the four provinces there: Volhynia, Kiev, Podolia, Kherson.

The Right Bank was also home for almost all the Poles living in the Dnieper Ukraine. They were most heavily represented in Volhynia, Kiev, and northern Poltava provinces and tended to inhabit the countryside and smaller towns in those regions. While numerically Poles increased during the nineteenth century—from 240,000 in 1795 to 656,000 in 1910—their proportion to the rest of the population in the Right Bank decreased—from 10 per cent in 1795 to 6.4 per cent in 1910.

The Germans first came to the Dnieper Ukraine in large numbers during the first decades of the nineteenth century. They came in response to tsarist decrees inviting them to settle (with various economic, social, and cultural privileges) in the Steppe Ukraine (southern Bessarabia, Kherson, Katerynoslav, and northern Taurida provinces) and the Crimea. Almost all these colonists, who came to be known as Black Sea Germans (*Schwarzmeerdeutsche*), settled in rural communities, each of which often consisted of a distinct religious group—Evangelical Lutherans, Catholics, or Mennonites. By 1897, there were 345,000 Black Sea Germans. Another group of Germans (almost all Evangelical Lutherans) began arriving in Volhynia in the 1860s and 1870s, where they rented or bought land from economically hard-pressed Polish nobles. By 1897, there were 170,000 Volhynian Germans.

Tatars had been living in the Crimea at least since their indepen-

dent khanate had come into existence during the fifteenth century. When the Crimea became part of the Russian Empire in 1783, there were an estimated 250,000 Tatars. Fearing the rule of their age-old enemy, 80,000 left for the Ottoman Empire before the end of the eighteenth century and another 30,000 departed during the first decades of the nineteenth century. The result was almost zero population growth, so that by 1897 there were 194,000 Tatars in the Crimea. Relative to the number of other inhabitants in the peninsula, their numbers fared worse. Before Russian rule, Tatars made up 90 per cent of the Crimean population; by 1913 they represented only 35 per cent.

Among the other minority populations in the Dnieper Ukraine were Romanians and Bulgarians in the rural areas of Kherson and southern Bessarabia; Greeks in the cities along the Black Sea and Sea of Azov coasts as well as in the rural steppe hinterland of Mariiupil'; and smaller numbers of Armenians in cities throughout all provinces.

In the Austro-Hungarian Empire, all three areas where Ukrainians lived—eastern Galicia (i.e., east of the San valley), northern Bukovina (i.e., north of the present day Soviet-Romanian border), and Transcarpathia—contained minority populations. Of the total population of 6,450,000 in these three areas in 1910, as many as 2,569,000 (39.9 per cent) were members of minorities. The largest of the minorities on Ukrainian lands in the Austro-Hungarian Empire were the Poles, Jews, and Germans.

TABLE II
Ethnic Composition of Ukrainian Lands (Eastern Galicia, Northern Bukovina, Transcarpathia) in the Austro-Hungarian Empire, 1910

Group	Number	Percentage
Ukrainians	3,881,000	60.1
Poles	1,381,000	21.4
Jews	823,000	12.7
Germans	125,000	1.9
Magyars	90,000	1.4
Romanians	87,000	1.3
Others	63,000	0.9
TOTAL	6,450,000	

(continued)

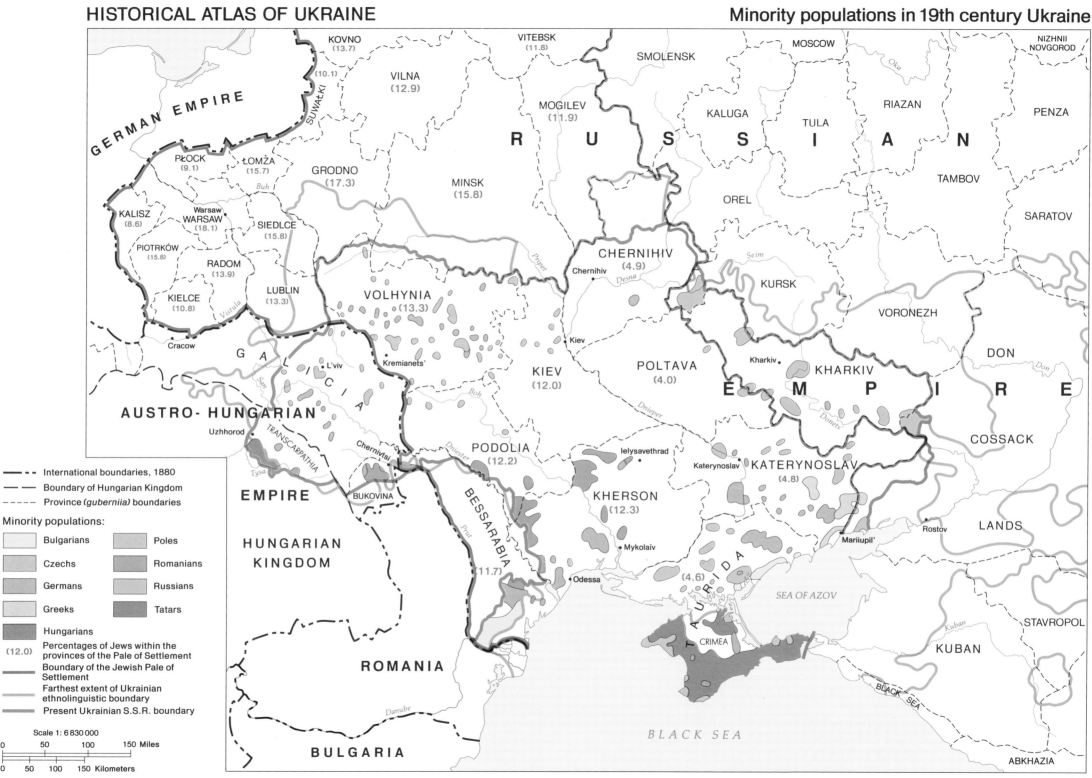

KOVNO
(13.7)

VITEBSK
(11.8)

MOSCOW

NIZHNII
NOVGOROD

SMOLENSK

(10.1)

SUWAŁKI

VILNA
(12.9)

MOGILEV
(11.9)

R U S S I A N

KALUGA

TULA

RIAZAN

PENZA

GERMAN EMPIRE

PŁOCK
(9.1)

ŁOMŻA
(15.7)

GRODNO
(17.3)

MINSK
(15.8)

OREL

TAMBOV

Buh

KALISZ
(8.6)

Warsaw
WARSAW
(18.1)

SIEDLCE
(15.8)

SARATOV

PIOTRKÓW
(15.8)

RADOM
(13.9)

LUBLIN
(13.3)

VOLHYNIA
(13.3)

Pripet

CHERNIHIV
(4.9)

Chernihiv

Seim

KURSK

KIELCE
(10.8)

Vistula

G A L I C I A

Cracow

L'viv

Kremianets'

Desna

Kiev

KIEV
(12.0)

POLTAVA
(4.0)

Kharkiv

KHARKIV

DON

Don

Donets

AUSTRO- HUNGARIAN

San

Boh

Dnieper

E M P I R E

Uzhhorod

TRANSCARPATHIA

Chernivtsi

PODOLIA
(12.2)

Ielysavethrad

Katerynoslav

KATERYNOSLAV
(4.8)

COSSACK

Dniester

Tysa

BUKOVINA

BESSARABIA

KHERSON
(12.3)

LANDS

EMPIRE

Mykolaïv

Rostov

HUNGARIAN
KINGDOM

(11.7)

Odessa

T A U R I D A
(4.6)

Mariiupil'

SEA OF AZOV

STAVROPOL

Prut

CRIMEA

KUBAN

Kuban

ROMANIA

BLACK SEA

BLACK SEA

Danube

ABKHAZIA

BULGARIA

Legend

- ·––·– International boundaries, 1880
- –––– Boundary of Hungarian Kingdom
- ------ Province (*guberniia*) boundaries

Minority populations:

	Bulgarians		Poles
	Czechs		Romanians
	Germans		Russians
	Greeks		Tatars
	Hungarians		

(12.0) Percentages of Jews within the provinces of the Pale of Settlement

Boundary of the Jewish Pale of Settlement

Farthest extent of Ukrainian ethnolinguistic boundary

Present Ukrainian S.S.R. boundary

Scale 1: 6 830 000

0   50   100   150 Miles

0   50   100   150 Kilometers

(map 18 continued)

MAP 19
The Austro-Hungarian Empire

The Poles lived in both rural and urban areas scattered throughout eastern Galicia. Whereas Poles have been entering the region ever since it had become part of the Polish Kingdom in the second half of the fourteenth century, it was during the nineteenth century that their increase was most dramatic. This growth was due both to natural demographic increases as well as to large-scale immigration from western Galicia. By 1910 there were over 1,351,000 Poles (i.e., Roman Catholics) in eastern Galicia and another 30,000 in northern Bukovina.

Like the Poles, Jews had also been living in eastern Galicia since at least the fourteenth century, and the most significant rise in their numbers also occurred during the nineteenth century as a result of a high birth rate and flight from pogroms in the neighboring Russian Empire. In 1850 there were 449,000 Jews throughout all of Galicia; by 1910 their numbers had almost doubled to 872,000. Three-quarters of them—660,000—lived in eastern Galicia, of whom as high as 76.2 per cent resided in cities and small towns. Jews were also found in the towns and small cities of northern Bukovina, where in 1910 they comprised 76,000 inhabitants (14.7 per cent of the total population), and in Transcarpathia, comprising about 87,000 inhabitants (14.5 per cent of the total population).

Although there were some Germans in Galicia in the Middle Ages, they had become assimilated by the sixteenth century. New waves of colonists came at the invitation of the Austrian government during the 1780s and the first half of the nineteenth century, so that by 1910 there were approximately 65,000 Germans in eastern Galicia. Most lived in small farming communities, especially in a belt running from north of L'viv southward to the Carpathian Mountains. Smaller numbers of Carpathian Germans (*Karpatendeutsche*), as they were known, lived in northern Bukovina—about 50,000, most especially in the administrative capital Chernivtsi—and in Transcarpathia—about 10,000 in a few villages.

Besides these groups, there were also about 87,000 Romanians living in the central lowland plains and in the city of Chernivtsi in northern Bukovina; 90,000 Magyars in the cities and lowland plains of southern Transcarpathia; and about 3,000 Armenians—remnants of a once vibrant medieval community—living in L'viv and a few other towns in eastern Galicia as well as in Bukovina.

During the nineteenth century Ukrainian lands were found within the borders of the Austrian (later Austro-Hungarian) Empire as well as in the Russian Empire. The Austrian Empire comprised a number of territories that in the course of several centuries had been acquired by its ruling Habsburg dynasty. The empire's greatest territorial extent was reached during the second half of the eighteenth century, when the Habsburgs ruled several regions of what later became northern Italy (Lombardy, Venetia, Tuscany, etc.), southern Germany, most of Belgium and Luxembourg (Austrian Netherlands), as well as the lands indicated by the international boundaries accompanying Map 19. Many of those territories were lost in the nineteenth century. During the last decades of that century, the only major territorial change came in 1878, with the addition of Bosnia-Herzegovina and the Sanjak of Novipazar. In 1908 Bosnia-Herzegovina was made an Austrian province and the Sanjak of Novipazar was returned to the Ottoman Empire.

The structure of the Austrian Empire was initially very complex, since each new territory acquired over the centuries—whether a kingdom, a grand duchy, a duchy, or simply a city—retained more often than not its own traditional customs and administration. The most distinct of these territories was the Hungarian Kingdom.

By the nineteenth century, efforts at administrative standardization resulted in the following binary structure for the Austrian Empire as a whole: (1) the Hungarian Kingdom and (2) the non-Hungarian lands, which together were ruled by a Habsburg who was both Austrian emperor and Hungarian king. The non-Hungarian part of the empire did not even have a name. Rather, it consisted of a conglomerate of historic provinces or crownlands (*Kronländer*), officially known as 'the kingdoms and crownlands represented in the imperial parliament.' By 1880 there were sixteen such kingdoms and crownlands, or provinces: Bohemia, Moravia, Silesia, Upper Austria, Lower Austria, Salzburg, Tyrol, Vorarlberg, Styria, Carniola, Trieste, Gorizia/Gradisca, Istria, Dalmatia, Galicia, and Bukovina—Bosnia-Herzegovina becoming the seventeenth province in 1908. Subsequent historical literature generally refers to these provinces together as Austria, or the Austrian half of the Habsburg Empire. After 1868, when the Hungarian Kingdom finally obtained virtual self-rule, the state as a whole came to be known as the Austro-Hungarian Empire or simply Austria-Hungary.

The Austro-Hungarian Empire was also known for the national complexity of its population. The Hungarian Kingdom and most of the Austrian provinces each contained several nationalities. Ukrainians lived basically in three areas of the empire: in the Austrian provinces of Galicia and Bukovina, and in the northeastern part of the Hungarian Kingdom.

NORTH
SEA

Hamburg

NETHERLANDS

Berlin

BELGIUM

GERMAN

LUX.

EMPIRE

FRANCE

Munich

SWITZERLAND

Rhine

Elbe

Oder

Vistula

Warsaw

WEST GALICIA
(1809)

Lublin

Pilica

Buh

RUSSIAN

EMPIRE

Kiev

Dnieper

Prague
(Prag)

Opava
(Troppau)

BOHEMIA

SILESIA

MORAVIA

Brno
(Brünn)

AUSTRIA-

Cracow
(Krakau)

G A L I C I A

L'viv
(Lemberg)

Dniester

Chernivtsi
(Czernowitz)

S L O V A K I A

Uzhhorod
(Ungvár)

TRANSCARPATHIA

BUKOVINA

Danube

Linz

LOWER

UPPER
AUSTRIA

AUSTRIA

Salzburg

Bratislava
(Pozsony/Pressburg)

Vienna

Tysa

Budapest

HUNGARIAN

KINGDOM

VORARLBERG

Innsbruck

SALZBURG

STYRIA

HUNGARY

Rhône

TYROL

CARINTHIA

Klagenfurt

Graz

GORIZIA-
GRADISCA

CARNIOLA

Ljubljana
(Laibach)

Drava

Zagreb
(Agram)

TRANSYLVANIA

LOMBARDY
(1859)

Milan
(Mailand)

VENETIA
(1866)

Venice

Trieste

ISTRIA

Rijeka
(Fiume)

Po

C R O A T I A - S L A V O N I A

ROMANIA

PARMA
(1847)

Parma

Modena

MODENA
(1860)

BOSNIA-
HERZEGOVINA

Belgrade

Bucharest

Danube

BLACK
SEA

LUCCA
(1847)

Florence

Zadar
(Zara)

DALMATIA

Sarajevo

SERBIA

TUSCANY
(1860)

CORSICA
(France)

Rome

A D R I A T I C   S E A

Dubrovnik
(Ragusa)

MONTENEGRO

SANJAK OF
NOVIPAZAR
(1908)

BULGARIA

TYRRHENIAN
SEA

ITALY

OTTOMAN EMPIRE

Constantinople

— · · — International boundaries, 1880
— — Boundary of Hungarian Kingdom
- - - - Austrian province boundaries (dates
         indicate when lost by Austria)
  ⊙ Provincial capitals
━━━ Ukrainian ethnolinguistic boundary
━━━ Present Ukrainian S.S.R. boundary

Scale 1: 7 320 000

0   100   200 Miles

0   100   200 Kilometers

MAP 20

Western Ukraine, 1772–1914

The western Ukraine comprises those lands within the Austro-Hungarian Empire where Ukrainians lived. These included parts of three regions: Galicia, Bukovina, and Transcarpathia. While Transcarpathia had been part of the Hungarian Kingdom and later Austrian Empire since the Middle Ages, it was not until 1772 that the Austrian part of the empire acquired significant numbers of Ukrainians. In that year, which saw the first partition of Poland, Austria obtained the Kingdom of Galicia and Lodomeria (usually shortened to Galicia), which included the Ukrainian-inhabited former Polish palatinates of Galicia (Rus') and Belz, as well as Polish-inhabited territory west of the San and south of the Vistula River.

Three years later, in 1775, Austria acquired the mountainous region of Bukovina from the Ottoman Empire, and in 1787 united it with Galicia. As a result of the third and final partition of Poland in 1795, Galicia's boundaries expanded northward to include most of the region between the Pilica, Vistula, and Buh rivers. This new territorial acquisition was known as West Galicia and remained under Austrian control until 1809, when it, together with the region around the city of Zamość, became part of the French-controlled Duchy of Warsaw, which in turn after 1815 became the Russian-controlled Congress Kingdom of Poland. After 1809 the Russian Empire also ruled the Ternopil' region (from the Zbruch River just to the west of the Seret River), which was returned to Austrian Galicia in 1815.

Ukrainians inhabited only parts of each of the three regions in question. They made up the majority of the population (71 per cent in 1849 and 63 per cent in 1910) in eastern Galicia, i.e., lands east of the San River valley. Ukrainians also lived in western Galicia along the slopes of the Carpathian Mountains—the Lemkian Region. In Bukovina, Ukrainians inhabited the northern half of the province, i.e., lands within the boundaries of the present-day Ukrainian SSR, where they comprised 58.3 per cent of the population in 1910. In Transcarpathia, Ukrainians inhabited the mountainous areas in the northern three-quarters of what is the present-day Transcarpathian Oblast of the Ukrainian SSR, as well as a strip of mountainous territory farther west—the so-called Prešov Region or southern Lemkian lands.

None of the Ukrainian lands within the Austro-Hungarian Empire had its own administration. Like other provinces in the Austrian half of the empire, Galicia was first divided into several regions (*Kreise*), and after 1867 into 74 and later 83 districts (*Bezirke*). The whole administration was headed by a governor and later a viceroy appointed by, and responsible to, the emperor in Vienna. The provincial capital and seat of the governor—and after 1861 an elected diet—was L'viv (Lemberg).

Bukovina formed one of the regions of Galicia until 1854. After several changes, it finally was made a separate province of Austria in 1861. It, too, was subdivided into districts (*Bezirke*) and ruled by a viceroy appointed by the emperor. Bukovina's administrative capital and after 1861 the seat of its provincial diet was Chernivtsi (Czernowitz).

Transcarpathia and other Ukrainian-inhabited lands to the west located in the Hungarian half of the empire were subdivided into several counties (*megye*). Each county was ruled by a lord-lieutenant appointed by, and responsible to, the Hungarian royal government in Budapest.

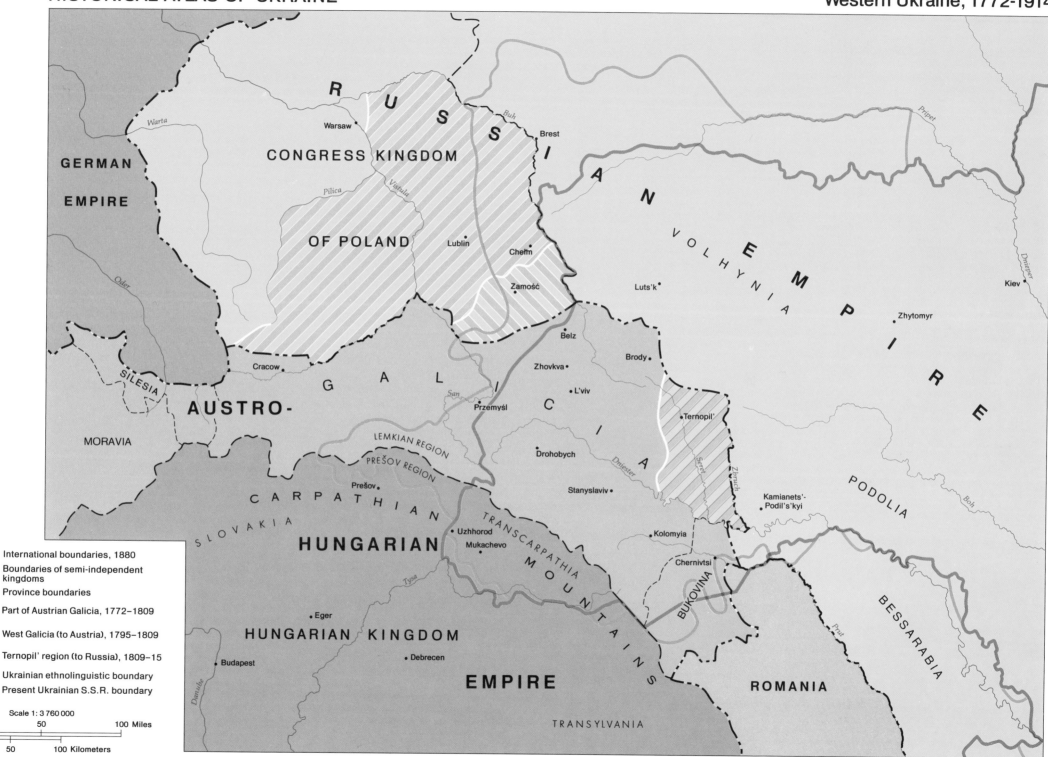

GERMAN

EMPIRE

R U S S I A N

CONGRESS KINGDOM

Warsaw

Brest

OF POLAND

Lublin

Chełm

Zamość

Belz

Luts'k

Brody

VOLHYNIA

Zhytomyr

E M P I R E

Kiev

Cracow

SILESIA

AUSTRO-

G A L I C I A

Zhovkva

L'viv

Przemyśl

Ternopil'

MORAVIA

LEMKIAN REGION

PREŠOV REGION

Drohobych

Dniester

CARPATHIAN

Prešov

Stanyslaviv

Kamianets'-
Podil's'kyi

PODOLIA

SLOVAKIA

HUNGARIAN

TRANSCARPATHIA

Uzhhorod

Mukachevo

Kolomyia

MOUNTAINS

Chernivtsi

BUKOVINA

BESSARABIA

Eger

HUNGARIAN KINGDOM

Debrecen

Budapest

EMPIRE

ROMANIA

TRANSYLVANIA

Warta
Pilica
Vistula
Buh
Pripet
Oder
San
Seret
Zbruch
Boh
Dnieper
Tysa
Danube
Prut

MAP 21

Ukrainian lands, 1914–1919

The outbreak of World War I in August 1914 ushered in a period that over five years later was to have a profound impact on the territorial disposition of Ukrainian lands. In the course of that half-decade, Ukrainian lands witnessed the military conflicts of World War I, the breakup of old empires, and several attempts to establish Ukrainian statehood, whether an independent non-Soviet state or a Soviet republic in close alliance with the new Soviet Russia. Moreover, all of these developments took place in an extremely complex environment marked by struggles between competing Ukrainian governments, peasant uprisings, foreign invasions, and civil war. If in 1914 Ukrainian lands were divided between two states, the multinational Russian and Austro-Hungarian empires, by early 1920 those empires had disappeared and most Ukrainians found themselves within the borders of four new states: the Ukrainian SSR, Poland, Czechoslovakia, and Romania.

The first administrative change came in western Ukrainian lands during the initial months of the war, when from the autumn of 1914 to the spring of 1915 the tsarist Russian army held most of Galicia (as far west as the Dunajec River) and Bukovina. By the summer of 1915 the tsarist troops and administration were driven out and the Austrians returned, although the Russians were able to hold on to a slice of Galician territory between the Seret and Zbruch rivers throughout most of the war.

The next major change came in 1917, this time in the Russian Empire, where the tsar was overthrown and his imperial rule replaced by that of a Provisional Government. By November of that same year, a second Russian revolution took place in which the Provisional Government was replaced by a Bolshevik-led government that called into being a Soviet Russian state.

Simultaneous with governmental changes in the Russian Empire, leaders in the Dnieper Ukraine formed a central council, or Rada, headed by Professor Mykhailo Hrushevs'kyi, and it set out to obtain autonomy and then independence for a Ukrainian state. In November 1917 and January 1918, the Central Rada proclaimed, respectively, the existence of an autonomous and then independent Ukrainian National Republic. Its territory was to comprise the nine 'Ukrainian' provinces from the former Russian Empire: Kiev, Volhynia, Podolia, Chernihiv, Poltava, Kharkiv, Katerynoslav, Kherson, and Taurida (excluding the Crimea). These nine provinces together with Chełm/Kholm and southern Grodno were recognized as part of the Ukrainian National Republic according to the provisions of the Treaty of Brest-Litovsk concluded in February 1918 with the Central Powers (Germany and Austria-Hungary), provisions subsequently accepted by Soviet Russia.

Despite this international recognition, the survival of the Central Rada and its Ukrainian National Republic was threatened from both east and west. At the end of 1917, Bolshevik forces claiming to represent a Soviet government of Ukraine invaded from the east; however, that government did not last long and, in the absence of any clear distinction from Soviet Russia, it did not delineate what specific territory it hoped to rule. On the other hand, the Central Rada's major ally from the west, Germany, beginning in April 1918, gave its support to a new government known as the Hetmanate. This pro-German Ukrainian government, headed by Hetman Pavlo Skoropads'kyi, remained in power until the end of 1918 and claimed all Ukrainian territory recognized by the Treaty of Brest-Litovsk as well as southern Minsk, southern Kursk, and southern Voronezh provinces and parts of the Don Cossack Lands.

Meanwhile, the western Ukrainian lands were directly affected by the disintegration of the Austro-Hungarian Empire and the imminent end to World War I. In such an atmosphere, Galician and Bukovinian leaders proclaimed in L'viv on 1 November 1918 the existence of a West Ukrainian People's Republic. This republic, headed by Ievhen Petrushevych, claimed as its territory all of Galicia east of the San River, including the Lemkian Region farther to the west and the Ukrainian-inhabited areas of Transcarpathia and northern Bukovina. In January 1919, the West Ukrainian People's Republic declared its unity with the Ukrainian National Republic which had been restored in Kiev after the fall of the Hetmanate government in December 1918. The restored Ukrainian National Republic, now led by Volodymyr Vynnychenko and Symon Petliura, claimed as its territory the boundaries of the Ukrainian state as previously outlined by the Treaty of Brest-Litovsk.

It should be kept in mind that despite the proclamations of these various Ukrainian governments, none ever exercised effective control over all the territories being claimed. This was particularly the case during 1919, when the conflicting interests of the various Ukrainian governments were complemented by invasions of the Bolsheviks, White Russians, Poles, and the Entente (the French occupied Odessa and the nearby coastal region); by almost continual peasant uprisings; and by general civil war—all of which resulted in virtual anarchy throughout the Ukraine.

By the end of 1920, the situation had finally begun to stabilize. A Bolshevik-led Soviet Ukrainian government (despite continual peasant uprisings, armed opposition of anti-Soviet Ukrainian forces, and an invasion by Poland) had gained control of most of the territory outlined as part of a Ukrainian Soviet Socialist Republic according to its constitution promulgated one year before (see Map 22). As for western Ukrainian lands, the Poles had already driven the West Ukrainian People's Republic out of Galicia (July 1919); the Romanians had taken over all of Bukovina (November 1918); and the Transcarpathians had decided to join the new state of Czechoslovakia (May 1919).

NIZHNII-
NOVGOROD

KOVNO
VITEBSK
SMOLENSK
MOSCOW

GERMAN EMPIRE

SUWAŁKI
Vilnius
VILNA
Smolensk
KALUGA
RIAZAN'
PENZA

PŁOCK
ŁOMŻA
GRODNO
Minsk
MINSK
Mahiloŭ
(Mogilev)
MOGILEV
TULA
TAMBOV
Tambov

KALISZ
WARSAW
Warsaw
SIEDLCE
Buh
R U S S I A N
OREL
SARATOV

PIOTRKÓW
Brest-Litovsk
Pinск
Pripet
Starodub
Kursk
Voronezh

RADOM
LUBLIN
CHEŁM
Chełm
Homel
CHERNIHIV
Desna
E M P I R E
DON

KIELCE
VOLHYNIA
Kiev
KURSK
VORONEZH

Cracow
G A Vistula
Przemyśl
L'viv
Zhytomyr
KIEV
POLTAVA
Kharkiv
KHARKIV
COSSACK

Dunajec
L I C I A
Ternopil'
Bila Tserkva
Dnieper
Poltava
Donets

LEMKIAN REGION
PREŠOV REGION
Prešov
Stanyslaviv
Seret
Zbruč
Vinnytsia
Kamianets'-
Podil's'kyi
PODOLIA
Katerynoslav
KATERYNOSLAV

AUSTRO-
Uzhhorod
TRANSCARPATHIA
San
Chernivtsi
Boh
KHERSON
Huliai-Pole
Taganrog
Rostov

Tysa
Khust
BUKOVINA
Dniester
Don

HUNGARIAN
BESSARABIA
Prut
Mykolaïv
LANDS

HUNGARIAN
Budapest
Odessa
STAVROPOL

EMPIRE
KINGDOM
TAURIDA
SEA OF AZOV
Kuban
KUBAN

CRIMEA

ROMANIA
Sevastopil'
BLACK SEA

Danube
BULGARIA
BLACK SEA
ABKHAZIA

International boundaries, 1914

Boundary of Hungarian Kingdom, 1914

Province boundaries, 1914

Ukraine after the Treaty of Brest-Litovsk, February, 1918

Territories claimed by Hetmanate, April–December, 1918

Territories claimed by the West Ukrainian Republic, 1918–19

Present Ukrainian S.S.R. boundary

Scale 1: 6 830 000

0   50   100   150 Miles

0   50   100   150 Kilometers

MAP 22
Ukrainian lands during the interwar years

The disposition of Ukrainian lands varied greatly during the interwar years depending on the administrative systems established in the four countries where Ukrainians lived: the Ukrainian SSR, Poland, Romania, and Czechoslovakia.

The Ukrainian SSR comprised the vast majority of the Dnieper Ukrainian lands that had previously belonged to the Russian Empire. These included most of the former nine 'Ukrainian' provinces from tsarist times, as well as the former Don Cossack Lands along the lower Donets' River valley and areas around Shakhty and Taganrog, but not western Volhynia and Chełm/Kholm which went to Poland or the non-Ukrainian inhabited portions of northern Chernihiv and southern Taurida which went, respectively, to the Russian SFSR and to the Crimean ASSR. Also, the Ukrainian-inhabited territories located in southern Kursk and Voronezh provinces as well as in the neighboring Don Cossack Lands and Kuban region went, respectively, to what later became the Central Russian oblast (with its center in Voronezh) and the Southwest oblast (with its center in Rostov) of the Russian SFSR. Ukrainian-inhabited southern Minsk (below the Pripet River in eastern Polissia) went to the Belorussian SSR.

Within the Ukrainian SSR itself, several administrative changes occurred during the interwar period. Initially, the nine 'Ukrainian' provinces (*guberniia*) of the old tsarist empire were maintained (see Map 21), although in 1920 three of them were subdivided, increasing the total number to twelve. Then, between 1923 and 1925, the old provinces were abolished and the whole territory of the Ukrainian SSR was divided into 53 *okruhs*, none of which had any relationship to a historical/territorial unit. Also, in 1924, a Moldavian Autonomous Soviet Socialist Republic was created along the lower Dniester River within the framework of the Ukrainian SSR. However, the Crimean ASSR had, since its creation in 1921, been within the framework of the Russian SFSR.

The number of *okruhs* in the Ukrainian SSR subsequently declined to 41, and two of them—Taganrog and Shakhty—were ceded in 1924 to the Russian SFSR. Several national districts were also created during the 1920s. The Germans had seven in the steppe and one each in Volhynia, the Donets' valley, and the Crimea; the Jews had three near Mykolaïv and two in the Crimea; the Poles had one just west of Zhytomyr.

In 1932 the administrative system of the Ukrainian SSR was changed once again. The *okruhs* were abolished and replaced by seven larger oblasts as indicated on the accompanying map: Chernihiv, Kiev, Vinnytsia, Kharkiv, Stalino, Dnipropetrovs'k, and Odessa. Each oblast was further divided into *raions* (districts), which in turn were composed of *silradas* (village councils). Later, new oblasts were created—Zhytomyr, Mykolaïv, Poltava, and Kamianets'-Podil's'kyi in 1937; Luhans'k in 1938; Zaporozhia, Kirovohrad, and Sumy in 1939—so that by the end of the interwar period the Ukrainian SSR was divided into 15 oblasts and 1 autonomous republic. The first capital of the Ukrainian SSR was Kharkiv; in 1934 Kiev became the capital.

As for Poland, it acquired Ukrainian-inhabited lands that had previously been part of the Austrian and Russian empires. After defeating the armies of the West Ukrainian People's Republic, Poland took over all of former Austrian Galicia in July 1919. The victorious Entente, which claimed sovereignty over Galicia, recognized Poland only as its temporary military occupant, but then in March 1923 recognized Polish sovereignty as well. With regard to the former tsarist-ruled Ukrainian-inhabited regions of western Volhynia, western Polissia, and southern Podlachia, Polish rule was accepted in the Treaty of Riga signed with Soviet Russia and Soviet Ukraine in March 1921.

In 1921 Poland was divided into palatinates (*województwa*), with virtually all of Volhynia (with its center at Luts'k), Ternopil', and Stanyslaviv as well as Polissia (with its center at Brest), eastern Lublin, and most of the L'viv palatinate being inhabited by Ukrainians. Although there had been some proposals regarding autonomy for former eastern Galicia—comprising the L'viv, Ternopil', and Stanyslaviv palatinates and known collectively as Eastern Little Poland (*Małopolska Wschodnia*)—the Polish government never granted any special administrative status to its Ukrainian-inhabited lands.

In Romania, Ukrainians lived in four areas: the very northern as well as southern coastal region of the former imperial Russian province of Bessarabia, the northern portion of the former Austrian province of Bukovina, and in a few villages located in what was the southeastern corner of the old Hungarian county of Maramarosh and the Danubian delta of northern Dobrudja. None of these areas had any special administrative status, and by the 1930s all had been subdivided into counties.

In Czechoslovakia, Ukrainians lived within two areas: the province of Subcarpathian Rus' (*Podkarpatská Rus*) and the northeastern corner of Slovakia, popularly known as the Prešov Region (*Priashivshchyna*). Subcarpathian Rus' had a special autonomous status within Czechoslovakia as guaranteed by the post-war peace treaties; and even if full autonomy was never granted, the territory did retain a distinct administrative status with its center at Uzhhorod throughout the interwar period.

GERMANY

Toruń

Biafystok

Nowogródek

Minsk

BELORUSSIAN

S.S.R.

Homel

U. S.

S. R.

Tambov

Kursk

Voronezh

Warsaw

Brest

Chernihiv

Desna

Sumy

Łódź

Lublin

POLAND

Chełm

POLISSIA

Pripet

Zhytomyr

Kiev

Kharkiv

Kielce

Luts'k

VOLHYNIA

Katowice

Vistula

San

Dnieper

Poltava

Donets'

Cracow

L'viv

GALICIA

Ternopil'

UKRAINIAN S.S.R.

LEMKIAN REGION

PRESOV REGION

Stanyslaviv

Vinnytsia

Luhans'k

CZECHOSLOVAKIA

SLOVAKIA

Uzhhorod

SUBCARPATHIAN RUS'

Dniester

Kamianets'-Podil'skyi

Boh

Kirovohrad

Dnipropetrovs'k

(to 1924)

Chernivtsi

BUKOVINA

Stalino

Shakhty

Budapest

Tysa

MARAMAROSH

BESSARABIA

MOLDAVIAN A.S.S.R.

Kryvyi Rih

Zaporozhia

Taganrog

Rostov

Don

HUNGARY

Prut

Mykolaïv

Kherson

R U S S I A N   S. F. S. R.

Odessa

SEA OF AZOV

KUBAN

Kuban

CRIMEAN A.S.S.R.

Symferopil'

ROMANIA

DOBRUDJA

Bucharest

Danube

BLACK SEA

BULGARIA

International boundaries, 1921

Soviet Socialist Republic boundaries

Autonomous Soviet Socialist Republic boundaries

Boundaries of Polish palatinates (1921), Czechoslovak provinces (1928), and Soviet oblasts (1932)

⊙ State capitals

⊙ Administrative centers of palatinates, provinces, and oblasts

Ukrainian ethnolinguistic boundary, 1930

Present Ukrainian S.S.R. boundary

Scale 1: 6 300 000

0   50   100   150 Miles

0   50   100   150 Kilometers

22

MAP 23

Ukrainian lands during World War II

Beginning in late 1938 and during the following six years, Ukrainian territories were progressively affected by the events of World War II that caused enormous physical and human destruction as well as frequent changes in administrations and international boundaries. The first changes occurred in the westernmost Ukrainian territory: Transcarpathia.

Following the German-imposed Munich Pact of September 1938, Czechoslovakia was transformed into a federal republic which granted to its easternmost province, Subcarpathian Rus' (Transcarpathia), its long-desired autonomy. The province was re-named Carpatho-Ukraine, but its autonomy proved to be short-lived. On 2 November 1938, Hungary was awarded the southern portion of Slovakia and of Carpatho-Ukraine (including its administrative center, Uzhhorod); five months later, on 15 March 1939, the Hungarians forcibly annexed the rest of Transcarpathia. Hungary was to rule Transcarpathia until September 1944, while during the same period Ukrainians living in northeastern Slovakia found themselves under the administration of a pro-German Slovak state.

The next territorial change occurred in Poland. As part of the August 1939 non-aggression pact between Nazi Germany and the Soviet Union, those two countries agreed to partition Ukrainian territories in Poland by a demarcation line that ran roughly along the San and Buh rivers. After Germany's invasion of Poland on 1 September 1939, precipitating World War II, Soviet forces moved in from the east. On 1 November 1939, the former Polish-held Ukrainian-inhabited lands of western Volhynia and eastern Galicia were accepted into the Ukrainian SSR, while western Polissia was joined to the Belorussian SSR. The Ukrainian-Belorussian border followed the present-day border between the two Soviet republics. As for Ukrainian-inhabited lands west of the German-Soviet demarcation line (i.e., southern Podlachia, the Chełm region, the Lemkian region), they became part of a German-ruled colony on former Polish territory known as the General-gouvernement.

Soviet Ukrainian borders expanded again in June 1940, when northern Bukovina was annexed from Romania, the new border following the present-day Soviet-Romanian boundary. At the same time, the Soviets also annexed from Romania neighboring Bes-sarabia: the very northern and southern regions were made part of the Ukrainian SSR; the larger central portion was joined to the Moldavian ASSR. The Moldavian ASSR was then separated jurisdictionally from the Ukrainian SSR and raised to republic status as the Moldavian SSR, its borders coinciding with the present-day Soviet Ukrainian–Soviet Moldavian boundary.

The Soviet presence on western Ukrainian territories was cut short by Germany's invasion of the Soviet Union beginning on 22 June 1941. Within five months, most of the Ukrainian SSR as far as Kharkiv and the Donets' River came under German control, while Germany's ally, Romania, was allowed to re-annex Bukovina and Bessarabia, and to acquire as well a region called Transnistria between the lower Dniester and Boh rivers (including Odessa). The farthest eastward advance of the German armies was attained in the summer of 1942, along a front following the course of the Don River and reaching Stalingrad on the Volga, and then southward beyond the Kuban region, thereby encompassing the entire Ukrainian SSR and most Ukrainian ethnolinguistic territory.

Behind the military zone along the eastern front, the Germans established three distinct administrative entities on Ukrainian lands. Eastern Galicia (that is, Galician lands east of the short-lived German-Soviet demarcation line) was made the fifth province (Distrikt Galizien) of the Generalgouvernement. Much of the rest of Ukrainian territory was reorganized into the so-called Reichskommissariat Ukraine, a German foreign colony with a German civil administrator resident in Rivne. The Crimea was ruled as a separate German foreign colony.

German, Romanian, and Hungarian rule on Ukrainian lands depended on the military situation. Following its success at the Battle of Stalingrad (November 1942 to February 1943), the Red Army advanced progressively westward. After defeating German troops and, most especially in the western Ukraine, anti-Soviet Ukrainian forces (the Ukrainian Revolutionary Army, UPA), the authority of the Ukrainian SSR was re-established. Most of 1943 witnessed the retreat of German forces from the Left Bank, Voroshylovhrad being the first Ukrainian city to be recaptured (14 February) and finally Kiev before the end of the year (6 November). During the winter and spring of 1944, the Germans were driven from the Crimea (April) and the Romanians from Trans-nistria (April) and northern Bukovina (March). By mid-summer (July-August), western Volhynia, western Polissia, and Galicia east of the Buh and San rivers were all in Soviet hands. Finally, by October 1944, the Red Army had driven the Hungarians out of Transcarpathia, a territory which was subsequently joined to the Ukrainian SSR following an agreement in June 1945 with Czechoslovakia (whose sovereignty over the region had until then been recognized by all the Allied Powers).

Ukrainian lands during World War II

BALTIC SEA
LATVIA
LITHUANIA
REICHSKOMMISSARIAT
OSTLAND
1941
DANZIG
GERMANY
Vilnius
Minsk
BELORUSSIAN
S.S.R.
Moscow
Smolensk
Oka
Western Dvina
CHUVASH A.S.S.R.
TATAR A.S.S.R.
Warta
Buh
PODLACHIA
Warsaw
Brest (July 28, 1944)
POLISSIA
Pripet
Desna
P O L A N D
1939
Chełm
GENERALGOUVERNEMENT
Cracow
Vistula
San
GALICIA
Przemyśl (July 27, 1944)
L'viv (July 27, 1944)
1941
VOLHYNIA
Rivne (Feb 5, 1944)
Brody (July 22, 1944)
REICHSKOMMISSARIAT
UKRAINE
Kiev (Nov 6, 1943)
Chernihiv (Sept 21, 1943)
Numbers shown in red indicate date of territorial acquisition.
Kursk
Voronezh
Don
Kharkiv (Aug 23, 1943)
Poltava (Sept. 23, 1943)
Dnieper
Donets
R U S S I A N S. F. S. R.
U. S. S. R.
Saratov
VOLGA GERMAN A.S.S.R. (to 1941)
Volga
Stalingrad
CZECHOSLOVAKIA
SLOVAKIA
Bratislava
Nov. 1938
Uzhhorod (Oct. 27, 1944)
March 1939
Dniester
Vinnytsia (March 20, 1944)
UKRAINIAN S.S.R.
1941
Voroshylovhrad (Feb 14, 1943)
Dnipropetrovs'k (Oct. 25, 1943)
Khust
CARPATHO-UKRAINE
Chernivtsi (March 30, 1944)
BUKOVINA
TRANSNISTRIA
Boh
MOLDAVIAN A.S.S.R.
1941
BESSARABIA
Prut
Budapest
Tysa
HUNGARY
1940
Cluj
TRANSYLVANIA
ROMANIA
Braşov
Bucharest
Danube
Odessa (April 10, 1944)
SEA OF AZOV
CRIMEAN A.S.S.R.
Sevastopil' (May 9, 1944)
KALMYK A.S.S.R. (to 1943)
Kuban
BLACK SEA
BULGARIA
GEORGIAN S.S.R.
International boundaries, 1938
Soviet Socialist Republic boundaries
Boundaries of Autonomous Soviet Socialist Republics
Boundaries of Czechoslovak provinces
German-Soviet demarcation line, September 1939–June 1941
Greater Germany, 1941
Other lands under German rule
Farthest German advance, November, 1942
Kiev (Nov 6, 1943) Ukrainian cities (with dates) recaptured by the Soviet Red Army
Ukrainian ethnolinguistic boundary
Present Ukrainian S.S.R. boundary
Scale 1: 8 000 000
0 100 200 Miles
0 100 200 Kilometers

MAP 24

The Ukrainian Soviet Socialist Republic since World War II

As a result of the Soviet victory in World War II, the boundaries of the USSR expanded westward. A total of 63,000 square miles that had before 1939 been part of Poland, Czechoslovakia, and Romania were now incorporated into the Ukrainian SSR. Similarily, most territory east of the Dniester River that before 1939 had been part of the Moldavian ASSR was made part of the Ukrainian SSR.

The international treaties that confirmed these territorial acquisitions awarded the USSR from Romania all of the old tsarist province of Bessarabia between the Prut and Dniester rivers as well as the northern half of old Austrian Bukovina. From Czechoslovakia came the province of Subcarpathian Rus' (Transcarpathia) according to its pre-1938 boundaries with only slight adjustments in the west (around Uzhhorod). From Poland came western Polissia, western Volhynia, and eastern Galicia. The new Polish-Soviet Ukrainian border followed approximately the so-called Curzon Line (proposed by a British minister after World War I), not the German-Soviet demarcation line of September 1939. This meant that Przemyśl and Ukrainian-inhabited territory in the upper San River valley were awarded to Poland.

On the new territories within the Ukrainian SSR, the Soviet administrative system according to oblasts was implemented. In fact, the oblasts that had already been created on most of these western Ukrainian territories under Soviet rule between 1939 and 1941 were simply restored after 1945. These included six oblasts on former Polish territory (Volhynia with its center at Luts'k, Rivne, Ternopil', Stanyslaviv, and L'viv and Drohobych east of the Curzon Line) and two oblasts on former Romanian territory (Chernivtsi and Izmaïl). As for former Czechoslovak territory, the Transcarpathian oblast was created (with its center at Uzhhorod), while former eastern Moldavian territory was joined to the Odessa oblast. The last territorial acquisition came when the Crimea—since 1945 demoted in status to an oblast of the Russian SFSR—was in 1954 given to the Ukrainian SSR, forming the Crimean oblast (with its center at Symferopil').

As during the interwar period, so too after 1945, did the administrative structure of the Ukrainian SSR continue to change. Besides the oblasts on newly acquired territory, Kherson was created in 1944 and Cherkasy in 1954, while Izmaïl was joined to Odessa in 1954 and Drohobych to L'viv in 1959. This means that since 1959 the territory of the Ukrainian SSR has been divided into 25 oblasts, which in turn are further divided (since 1968) into 475 *raions* (districts), 382 cities, 827 rural towns, and 32,043 rural villages.

Eighty per cent of contiguous Ukrainian ethnolinguistic territory lies within the boundaries of the Ukrainian SSR, and 87 per cent of all Ukrainians live there; the remainder live in neighboring Soviet republics and countries. Within the USSR, Ukrainians inhabit parts of the Brest and Homel oblasts of the Belorussian SSR; parts of the Briansk, Kursk, Belgorod, Voronezh, Rostov, and Volgograd oblasts and the Krasnodar and Stavropol lands (*krai*) of the Russian SFSR; and small areas in the northernmost and eastern edges of the Moldavian SSR.

Outside the USSR, contiguous Ukrainian ethnolinguistic territory is found in three countries: in Poland, along the eastern edges of the Białystok, Biała Podlaska, Chełm, Zamość, and Przemyśl palatinates and along the southern edges of the Krosno and Nowy Sącz palatinates; in Czechoslovakia, in several districts (*okresy*) in the northeastern part of the East Slovak Land (*kraj*), popularly known as the Prešov Region (*Priashivshchyna*); and in Romania, in the northernmost sections of the counties (*oblasts*) of Maramureş (with its center at Baia Mare), Suceava, and Dobrudja (with its center at Constanţa).

LATVIAN S.S.R.

BALTIC SEA

LITHUANIAN
S.S.R.

Nieman

Western Dvina

• Kalinin

• Vladimir

• Moscow

R
U
S
S
I
A
N

CHUVASH
A.S.S.R.

TATAR
A.S.S.R.

• Ulianovsk

• Gdańsk

R.S.F.S.R.

Vilnius ⊙

Vitebsk •

Smolensk •

Oka

Riazan •

• Gorky

MORDOVIAN
A.S.S.R.

POLAND

• Grodno

Minsk ⊙

Mahiloŭ
(Mogilev) •

BELORUSSIAN

S.S.R.

Kaluga •

• Tula

• Penza

Biafystok •

Briansk •

S.

• Saratov

Warsaw ⊙

Buh

Biała
Podlaska •

• Brest

Pinsk •

Pripet

Homel •

U.

Desna

• Orel

S.

Chernihiv •

• Kursk

S.

• Voronezh

R.

Volga

S.

Chefm •

Zamość •

Luts'k ⊙

• Rivne

Zhytomyr •

Kiev ⊙

Sumy •

• Belgorod

F.

Cracow •

Vistula

San

Nowy
Sącz • Krosno • Przemyśl •

L'viv ⊙

UKRAINIAN

S.S.R.

Kharkiv •

S.

CZECHOSLOVAKIA

Prešov •

Drohobych •

Ternopil' •

Khmel'nyts'kyi •

Poltava •

Donets'

R.

KAZAKH
S.S.R.

Uzhhorod ⊙

Ivano-
Frankivs'k
(Stanyslaviv) •

Vinnytsia •

Cherkasy •

Dnieper

Voroshylovhrad •

• Budapest

Chernivtsi •

Dniester

Kirovohrad •

Dniipropetrovs'k •

Donets'k •

• Volgograd

HUNGARY

Tysa

Baia Mare •

Suceava •

MOLDAVIAN
S.S.R.

Prut

Boh

Zaporozhia •

Don

Kishinev ⊙

Mykolaiv •

Rostov •

KALMYK
A.S.S.R.

ROMANIA

Odessa •

Kherson •

SEA OF AZOV

• Elista

Kuban

Bucharest ⊙

Danube

Izmaïl •

Krasnodar •

• Stavropol

DAGESTAN
A.S.S.R.

BULGARIA

• Constanța

Symferopil' •

BLACK SEA

KABARDINO-
BALKAR
A.S.S.R.

CHECHINO-
INGUSH
A.S.S.R.

N. OSSETIAN
A.S.S.R.

GEORGIAN S.S.R.

Legend

—·—·— International boundaries, 1985

——— Soviet Socialist Republic boundaries

- - - - Autonomous Soviet Socialist
Republic boundaries

·········· Oblast boundaries

⊙ State capitals

• Oblast administrative centers

——— Ukrainian ethnolinguistic boundary

Scale 1: 8 000 000

0   100   200 Miles

0   100   200 Kilometers

GAZETTEER

The grid numbers refer to
the accompanying map;
the numbers in parentheses refer
to other maps in the volume.

Akkerman, C-4 (10)
Azov, E-4 (10, 14, 15)

Baia Mare, A-4 (24)
Bakhchesarai, D-5 (10, 12–15)
Bakhmut, E-3 (15)
Balaklava, D-5 (10)
Balta, C-4 (15, 17)
Bar, B-3 (15)
Batih, C-3 (13)
Baturyn, D-2 (14)
Bazavluk (11)
Belgorod, E-2 (13–15, 24)
Belz, B-2 (8, 10, 20)
Belz (region), B-2 (13–15)
Bendery, C-4 (15)
Berestechko, B-2 (13)
Bessarabia, B-4, C-4, C-5 (1, 2, 17, 18, 20–23)
Biała Podlaska, A-1 (24)
Białystok, A-1 (24)
Bila Tserkva, C-3 (1, 2, 13–15, 21)
Bilhorod, C-4 (8)
Bil's'ke, D-2 (3)
Black Sea Lands, C-4, D-4 (1, 2)
Boikian Region, A-3 (2)
Bospor, see Panticapaeum
Braşov, B-5 (23)
Bratslav, C-3 (10, 13–15)
Bratslav (region), C-3 (10, 13–15)
Brest, A-1 (1, 2, 8–10, 12, 13, 17, 20–24)
Brest-Litovsk, A-1 (21)
Briansk, D-1 (12, 24)
Brody, B-2 (20, 23)
Bucharest, B-5 (1, 2, 22–24)
Bukovina, B-3, B-4 (1, 2, 15, 17–23)

Caffa (Kefe), D-5 (9, 10, 12)
Carpatho-Ukraine, see Transcarpathia
Cembalo, D-5 (9)
Chełm (Kholm), A-2 (1, 2, 8, 10, 12, 14, 15, 17, 20–24)
Chełm (region), A-2 (21)
Cherkasy, D-3 (1, 2, 10, 13, 14, 24)
Chernihiv, C-2 (1, 2, 5–10, 12–15, 17, 18, 22–24)

Chernihiv (region), C-2, D-1, D-2 (7–10, 13, 17, 18, 21)
Chernivtsi, B-3 (1, 2, 18–24)
Chersonesus, D-5 (3–7)
Cherven (Czerwień), A-2 (6, 8)
Chyhyryn, D-3 (10, 13–15)
Cluj, A-4 (23)
Constanţa, C-5 (24)
Crimea, D-5 (1–3, 9, 11, 15, 17, 18, 21)
Czerwień, see Cherven

Debrecen, A-4 (20)
Derman', B-2 (12)
Dnipropetrovs'k, D-3 (1, 2, 22–24)
Dobrudja, C-5 (22)
Donbas, E-3 (1, 2)
Donets'k, E-3 (1, 2, 24)
Doros, D-5 (4)
Drohobych, A-3 (20, 24)
Dryzhypole, C-3 (13)
Dubno, B-2 (12)

Ekaterinodar, see Krasnodar
Ekaterinoslav, see Katerynoslav

Feodoro, see Mangup

Galicia, A-2, A-3, B-3 (1, 2, 7–10, 13–15, 17–23)
Gözlere, see Ievpatoriia

Hadiach, D-2 (13–15)
Halych, B-3 (6–10, 12)
Hermanossa (Tamatarcha), E-5 (3)
Hetmanate, C-2, D-2, D-3 (14, 15)
Hlukhiv, D-2 (13–15)
Homel, C-1 (21, 22, 24)
Horodok, A-3 (12)
Huliai-Pole, E-4 (21)

Iaroslav, see Jarosław
Ielysavethrad, D-3 (15, 17, 18)
Ievpatoriia (Gözleve), D-5 (10)
Iskorosten', C-2 (5)
Iuzivka, see Stalino
Ivano-Frankivs'k (Stanyslaviv), B-3 (24)
Izium, E-3 (14, 15)
Izmaïl, C-5 (24)

Jarosław (Iaroslav), A-2 (8)
Jassy, B-4 (10, 12, 13)

Kal'nyk, C-3 (13)
Kamianets'-Podil's'kyi, B-3 (10, 12, 14, 17, 20–22)

Kamians'ke, D-4 (3)
Kaniv, C-3 (13)
Katerynoslav, D-3 (15, 17, 18, 21)
Kefe, see Caffa
Kharkiv, E-3 (1, 2, 15, 17, 18, 21–24)
Kherson, D-4 (15, 17, 22, 24)
Khmel'nyts'kyi, B-3 (24)
Kholm, see Chełm
Khotyn, B-3 (10, 17)
Khust, A-3 (21, 23)
Kiev, C-2 (1–10, 12–14)
Kiev (region), C-2, C-3 (7–10, 13–15, 17, 18, 21)
Kiliia, C-5 (10)
Kirovohrad, D-3 (22, 24)
Kishinev, C-4 (24)
Kodak, D-3 (10, 11, 13, 14)
Kolomyia, B-3 (20)
Konotop, D-2 (13)
Korsun', C-3 (10, 13)
Košice, A-3 (8)
Krasnodar, E-5 (1, 2, 24)
Kremianets', B-2 (18)
Kropyvna, D-3 (13)
Krosno, A-3 (24)
Kryvyi Rih, D-4 (1, 2, 17, 22)
Kuban Region, E-5 (1, 2, 18, 21, 22)
Kursk, E-2 (1, 2, 8, 15, 17, 21–24)

Lemkian Region (Lemkivshchyna), A-3 (2, 20–22)
Lithuania (region), B-1, C-1 (10, 12–15)
Liubech, C-2 (7, 8)
Lublin, A-2 (9, 10, 12, 17, 19, 20, 22)
Lubny, D-2 (10, 13–15)
Luhans'k, E-3 (22)
Luts'k, B-2 (8, 10, 12, 15, 20, 22, 24)
L'viv, B-3 (1, 2, 8–10, 12–24)

Mangup, D-5 (9)
Maramarosh, A-4, B-4 (22)
Mariiupil', E-4 (17, 18)
Matrega, E-5 (9)
Mazovia, A-1 (9, 10, 14, 15)
Moldavia, see Stalino
Moldavia (region), B-4 (10, 12–15, 17)
Moncastro, C-4 (9)
Mukachevo, A-3 (12, 14, 20)
Mykolaïv, D-4 (1, 2, 17, 18, 21, 22, 24)
Mykytyn Rih (11)
Myrhorod, D-3 (13, 15)

Neapolis, D-5 (3)
Nemyriv, C-3 (12)
Nemyrivs'ke, C-3 (3)
Nizhyn, C-2 (13–15)

Nova Sich, D-4 (11, 15)
Novhorod-Sivers'kyi, D-1 (7–9)
Novomyrhorod, C-3 (15)

Ochakiv, C-4 (14)
Odessa, C-4 (1, 2, 15, 17, 18, 21–24)
Okhtyrka, D-2 (13–15)
Olbia, C-4 (3, 4)
Oleshky, D-4 (11, 15)
Ostrih, B-2 (10, 12)
Ostrogozhsk, E-2 (15)
Ovruch, 2-C (12, 13)

Panticapaeum (Bospor), E-5 (3, 4)
Pavoloch, C-3 (13)
Pereiaslav, C-2 (7, 8, 10, 13–15)
Peremyshl', see Przemyśl
Peresichen', C-4 (5)
Phanagoria, E-5 (3)
Pinsk, B-1 (1, 2, 7–8, 12, 17, 21)
Pochaïv, B-2 (12)
Podlachia (Pidliashshia), A-1, A-2, (1, 2, 9, 10, 13–15, 22, 23)
Podolia (Podillia), B-3, C-3 (1, 2, 9, 10, 13–15, 17, 18, 20, 21)
Pokuttia, B-3 (2)
Polissia, B-2, C-2 (1, 2, 22, 23)
Poltava, D-3 (1, 2, 13–15, 17, 20–24)
Prešov, A-3 (20, 21, 24)
Prešov Region (Priashivshchyna), A-3 (20, 22)
Proskuriv, see Khmel'nyts'kyi
Pryluky, D-2 (13, 15)
Przemyśl (Peremyshl'), A-3 (1, 2, 5, 6, 8–10, 12, 14, 15, 17, 20, 21, 23, 24)
Putyvl', D-2 (8, 13, 14)
Pyliavtsi, B-3 (13)

Rivne, B-2 (23, 24)
Rohatyn, B-3 (12)
Rostov, E-4 (1, 2, 17, 18, 21, 22, 24)

Sandomierz, A-2 (8)
Sevastopil', D-5 (1, 2, 23)
Shakhty, F-4 (22)
Sich (11)
Skyt Maniavs'kyi, B-3 (12)
Sloboda Ukraine, D-2, E-2 (1, 2, 13–15)
Slutsk, B-1 (12)
Soldaia, D-5 (9)
Solkhat, D-5 (9, 10)
Stalino, E-3 (22)
Stanyslaviv, B-3 (20–22, 24)
Stara Sich, D-4 (11, 13–15)
Starodub, D-1 (9, 10, 12–15, 21)
Subcarpathian Rus', see Transcarpathia

Suceava, B-4 (9, 12, 24)
Sugdea, D-5 (8)
Sumy, D-2 (15, 22, 24)
Symferopil', D-5 (17, 22, 24)

Taganrog, E-4 (17, 21, 22)
Tamatarcha, see Hermanossa
Tana, E-4 (9)
Tanais, E-4 (3, 4)
Terebovlia, B-3 (8)
Ternopil', B-3 (12, 20–22, 24)
Theodosia, D-5 (3)
Tiras, C-4 (3, 4)
Tmutorokan, E-5 (5–8)
Tomakivka (11)
Transcarpathia (Carpatho-Ukraine, Subcarpathian Rus'), A-3, B-3 (1, 2, 9, 15, 17–23)
Transnistria, C-3, C-4 (23)
Transylvania (region), A-4, B-4 (10, 12, 14, 19, 20, 23)
Turov, B-1 (7–9, 12)

Uman', C-3 (13–15)
Univ, B-3 (12)
Uzhhorod, A-3 (1, 2, 17–24)

Vinnytsia, C-3 (13, 21–24)
Volhynia, B-2, C-2 (1, 2, 7–10, 13–15, 17, 18, 20–23)
Volodymyr, B-2 (6–10, 12)
Volyn', B-2 (5)
Voronezh, E-2 (1, 2, 13–15, 17, 21–24)
Voroshylovhrad, E-3 (23, 24)
Vosporo, E-5 (9)

Wallachia, A-5, B-5 (9, 10, 12–15, 17)
Warsaw, A-1 (1, 2, 10, 12–15, 17–24)

Yalta, D-5 (1, 2)

Zabłudów (Zabludiv), A-1 (12)
Zamość (Zamostia), A-2 (13, 20, 24)
Zaporozhia (Zaporizhzhia), D-4 (1, 2, 22, 24)
Zaporozhia (region), D-3, D-4, E-3 (1, 2, 10, 12–15)
Zboriv, B-3 (13)
Zhdanov, E-4 (2)
Zhovkva, A-2 (12, 20)
Zhovti Vody, D-3 (13)
Zhvanets', B-3 (13)
Zhydychyn, B-2 (12)
Zhytomyr, C-2 (1, 2, 17, 20–22, 24)
Zvenyhorod, B-3 (8)

SOURCES

Atlas Historyczny Polski, ed. Władysław Czapliński and Tadeusz Ładogórski. Warsaw: Państwowe przedsiębiorstwo wydawnictw kartograficznych, 1970

Atlas östliches Mitteleuropa, ed. Theodor Kraus. Bielefeld, Berlin, and Hanover: Velhagen und Klasing, 1959

Atlias Ukraïny i sumezhnykh kraïv, ed. Volodymyr Kubiiovych. L'viv: Ukraïns'kyi vydavnychyi instytut for the Naukove tovarystvo imeni Shevchenka, 1937

Bieńkowski, Ludomir et al. *Kościół w Polsce*, Vol. II: *wieki XVI–XVII*. Cracow: ZNAK, 1970, map supplements

Encyklopedia powszechna PWN, Vol. III. Warsaw: Państwowe Wydawnictwo Naukowe, 1975, 'Polska: mapy'

Entsyklopediia ukraïnoznavstva: slovnykova chastyna, 8 vols. [A–Ty], ed. Volodymyr Kubiiovych. Paris and New York: Molode zhyttia for the Naukove Tovarystvo im. Shevchenka, 1955–76

Grosser historischer Weltatlas, 3 vols., ed. Josef Engel. 3rd edition. Munich: Bayerischer Schulbuch-Verlag, 1967

Historia Polski, ed. Tadeusz Manteuffel. Vol. I: *Mapy do roku 1764,* and Vol. II: *Mapy do roku 1864*. Warsaw: Państwowe Wydawnictwo Naukowe, 1958–60

Istoriia Ukraïns'koï RSR, 8 vols. in 10, ed. A.H. Sheveliev and Iu. Iu. Kondufor. Kiev: Naukova dumka, 1977–79

Kubijovyč, V. and Žukovs'kyj, A. *Ukraïna: karta Ukraïny*. Munich and Paris: Knyha Vlg., 1978

Kyïv: istorychnyi ohliad (karty, iliustratsiï, dokumenty), ed. A.V. Kudryts'kyi. Kiev: Holovna redaktsiia Ukraïns'koï radians'koï entsyklopediï, 1982

The New Cambridge Modern History, Vol. XIV: *Atlas*, ed. H.C. Darby and Harold Fullard. Cambridge: Cambridge University Press, 1970; reprinted with corrections 1978

Ocherki istorii SSSR, ed. B.D. Grekov and N.M. Druzhinin, 7 vols. [III–XVIII vv.]—*karty*. Moscow: Akademiia nauk SSSR, 1953–58

Radians'ka entsyklopediia istoriï Ukraïny, 4 vols., ed. A.D. Skaba et al. Kiev: Holovna redaktsiia Ukraïns'koï Radians'koï entsyklopediï, 1969–72

Teslia, Ivan and Tiut'ko, Evhen. *Istorychnyi atlas Ukraïny*. Montreal, New York, and Munich: Ukraïns'ke istorychne tovarystvo, 1980

Ukraine: A Concise Encyclopedia, 2 vols., ed. Volodymyr Kubijovyč. Toronto: University of Toronto Press for the Ukrainian National Association, 1963–71